A 1940s Monadnock CHILDHOOD

A 1940s *Monadnock* CHILDHOOD

Tom Shultz

THE History PRESS

Published by The History Press
Charleston, SC 29403
www.historypress.net

Images are courtesy of the author unless otherwise noted.

Cover images: Mount Monadnock, framed by a stone wall and sugar maples from the Dublin side. *Courtesy of Baxter Harris, Smiling Dog Productions*; Peterborough Pool. *Collection of the Peterborough Historical Society*; Peterborough High School basketball team (1945–46). *Collection of the Peterborough Historical Society.*

First published 2011

Manufactured in the United States

ISBN 978.1.60949.265.6

Library of Congress Cataloging-in-Publication Data

Shultz, Tom.
A 1940s Monadnock childhood / Tom Shultz.
p. cm.
Includes bibliographical references.
ISBN 978-1-60949-265-6
1. Peterborough (N.H.)--Social life and customs. 2. Peterborough (N.H.)--History. 3. Peterborough (N.H.)--Biography. 4. Monadnock, Mount, Region (N.H.)--Social life and customs. 5. Monadnock, Mount, Region (N.H.)--History. 6. Monadnock, Mount, Region (N.H.)--Biography. 7. Shultz, Tom--Homes and haunts. I. Title.
F44.P4S58 2011
974.2'9--dc23
2011030452

This book is dedicated to the memory of Peggy, my wife of forty-five years. Without her encouragement, patience and countless hours on the computer, printing the manuscript, and her comprehension of manuscript format, this book could not have been written. She also had a keen eye for correct punctuation and spelling.

Would that Peggy were here to witness her efforts become reality.

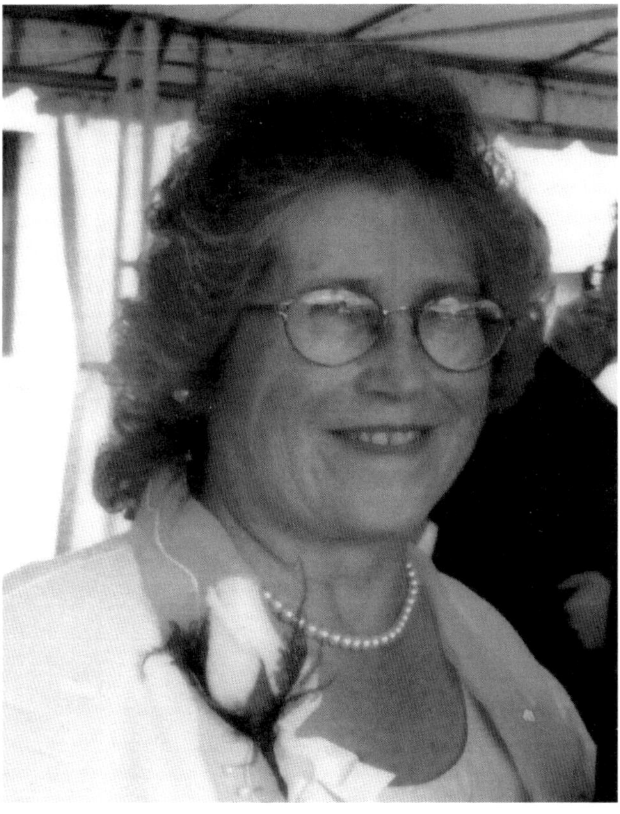

Contents

Preface

This book is not about the life and times of the author; rather, it is a chronicle of the people, places and events that took place during that era. Actually, this span is a narrow window of time, which began when we moved to Peterborough from Ames, Iowa, in November 1937. It ended with the graduation of the class of 1950 from Peterborough High School in early June 1950.

Why would anybody want to read a book I have written? I'm certainly not famous. I do not have name recognition, don't possess intellectual credentials and am not a sports or entertainment personality or a politician. I'm known only to family, friends and acquaintances.

In my view, I think people enjoy reading about other people to whom they can relate. We've all grown up with dreams, hopes and aspirations, and hopefully readers can relate to what I've written about growing up in a small southern New Hampshire town.

I would like to think that readers will say to themselves, "Oh, yes, I remember those events," "That's just the way it was" or "Here I thought I was the only one who enjoyed those times." My special wish is for them to say, "I never realized the uniqueness of Peterborough."

I do appear in cameo roles from time to time, relating my experiences growing up in Peterborough from 1937 to 1950. I underscore the point that no attempt has been made to compare "Our Town" back then to twenty-first-century Peterborough, because this narrative is strictly from an objective point of view.

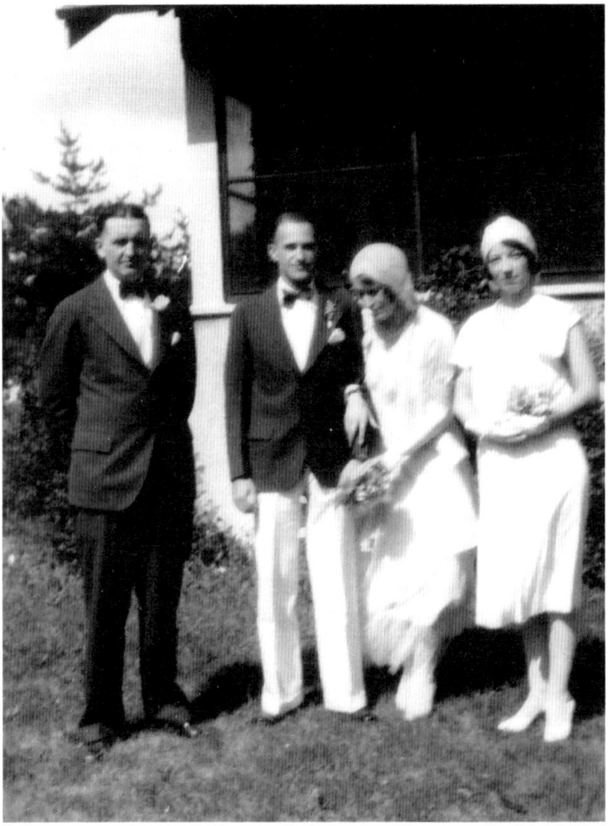

Earl and Helen Shultz on their wedding day, July 16, 1930, in the depths of the Great Depression.

My role is like that of a raconteur, standing on the sidelines, recounting the happenings and events that took place back then. Those of us who remember that era are literally a dying breed, and unless there is a written account, how will anybody living in the twenty-second century learn what took place back then? Hopefully, they will be as interested then as we are now regarding the history of Peterborough and the Monadnock region.

Historically, this was an eventful era. Our country had recovered from the Great Depression of the 1930s, during which time our parents had married, entered into the workforce and raised their families. Then World War II engulfed the entire world in a horrendous battle between the United States, its allies and the Axis powers. The cost in human lives and suffering was astronomical: the United States armed forces suffered 292,131 deaths and 671,846 wounded. World War II galvanized all Americans in a common cause to preserve their Four Freedoms.

The Imperial Navy of Japan attacked Pearl Harbor on December 7, 1941. On December 8, at the request of President Roosevelt, Congress passed a joint resolution, with one dissenting vote, stating that war existed between the United States and Japan. President Roosevelt approved the resolution and was authorized to deploy our armed forces in combat against Japan. The president proclaimed, "We're going to win the war, and we are going to win the peace that follows."

Germany and Italy declared war on the United States on December 11. Congress passed a resolution, with no dissenting votes, stating that the United States was officially at war with Germany and Italy. President Roosevelt approved and signed this resolution. The United States was now embroiled in World War II.

After three years and eight months, World War II ended with the unconditional surrender of the Axis powers. President Roosevelt had made good on his promise to win the war; now he would fulfill the covenant to win the peace.

Secretary of State George C. Marshall—who devised the Marshall Plan, or European Recovery Program, for which he received the Nobel Peace Prize in 1953—accomplished this promise. When Marshall resigned his position for health reasons, Secretary of State Dean Acheson implemented the plan. Under the leadership of General Douglas MacArthur, a similar recovery and reconstruction plan was implemented in Japan.

During the postwar era, millions of military veterans returned to civilian life. Some obtained college educations or vocations under the GI Bill; others bought homes for their families or became small businessmen with GI loans.

Industries retooled from manufacturing war materials to producing consumer goods. This transition was neither easy nor instantaneous. Making a change from the frenzy of a wartime economy to that of a peaceful consumer way of life required time and patience. Returning veterans wanted to put the war behind them and get on with their civilian lives.

Acknowledgements

Though my name appears on the book's cover, many individuals have made valuable contributions to its publication.

My son Mike, with his wealth of computer skills, comprehension of the Internet and knowledge of computer printout and image scanning, was an invaluable asset. Without his assistance, this book would never have seen the light of day. He gave up family time to do so, for which Dad is eternally grateful.

My son Joe also assisted by e-mailing Mike information regarding Monadnock region towns.

My classmate Jan Currier Caskey was instrumental in making this book a reality. She obtained for me a brochure from The History Press outlining its publication objectives, authors' guidelines and manuscript proposal process. In telephone conversations, Jan provided local items of interest regarding Hancock.

Dotty Dole Johnson was so helpful in providing me with insight through numerous conversations regarding the Dole family and events in the Monadnock region during the 1940s. Dotty gave me both editions of the *History of Peterborough*, written by George A. Morison and Miss Etta M. Smith. These books are a treasure-trove of information, and I'm so grateful to have them. She also provided pictures of the Dole family and homestead.

Many thanks to classmates Bob Clark, Don Colburn and Tom Day for contributing pictures shown in this book.

Ms. Michelle Stahl, executive director of the Peterborough Historical Society, was most helpful in providing images of the Monadnock region.

Ms. Katherine Schillemat, administrative assistant at the Historical Society of Cheshire County, provided factual backgrounds for towns in the Monadnock region.

Brian Haskert, reference librarian at Peterborough Library, provided images of Peterborough landmarks.

Ms. Polly S. Cote provided information regarding Milford, another town in the Monadnock region.

Molly Backup captured on film a typical Vermont Yankee—her grandfather, Mr. Fletcher Dole.

The image of my wife, Peggy, on the dedication page was provided by her brother-in-law, Paul Robinson, who was also the photographer.

I would also like to thank the following businesses for their help:

Baxter Harris of Smiling Dog Productions, Windy Row, Peterborough. His photo of Mount Monadnock defined the very heart and soul of the Monadnock region. Dr. Donald H. Fritz, veterinarian and longtime friend, provided the image to me.

The Coughlin Printing Group, Lowville, New York, for providing typing services and file formatting.

Urbaniak Studio and Color Lab, Lowville, New York, for providing image digitization and photo reproductions.

The Warren Kay Vantine Studio, Boston, Massachusetts, for providing the class of 1950 picture.

Monadnock Region

The Grand Lady Mount Monadnock, which means "standing alone" in the Souhegan Penacook Indian language, is the prominent geographical feature viewed when approaching the Monadnock region. Her presence declares, "Welcome, daughters and sons; after a weary journey, you are finally home in the Monadnock region."

Though the main locale of this book is Peterborough, it has much in common with neighboring towns in the Monadnock region. The major common bond is the prominence of Mount Monadnock. Though not tall by any means at 3,165 feet above sea level, only Mount Fuji in Japan has attracted more climbers over the years.

Monadnock has been a magnet, attracting prominent composers, writers and artists to Peterborough, Dublin, Jaffrey and Hancock.

Edward MacDowell, noted composer and pianist, and his wife, Marian, established MacDowell Colony in Peterborough. *Amos Fortune—Free Man* was a biography written by Elizabeth Yates, a resident of Peterborough who chose Jaffrey as the locale for this 1951 Newberry Medal winner. Amos Fortune was an African-born slave who came to America and then won his freedom from Ichabod Richardson, a tanner. Amos settled in Jaffrey and himself became a skilled tanner, noted for his craftsmanship.

Spending summers at the Shattack Inn in Jaffrey, Willa Cather was inspired to finish the novel *My Antonia*; several other books of hers were partially written here as well. Writer P.J. O'Rourke resided in Jaffrey.

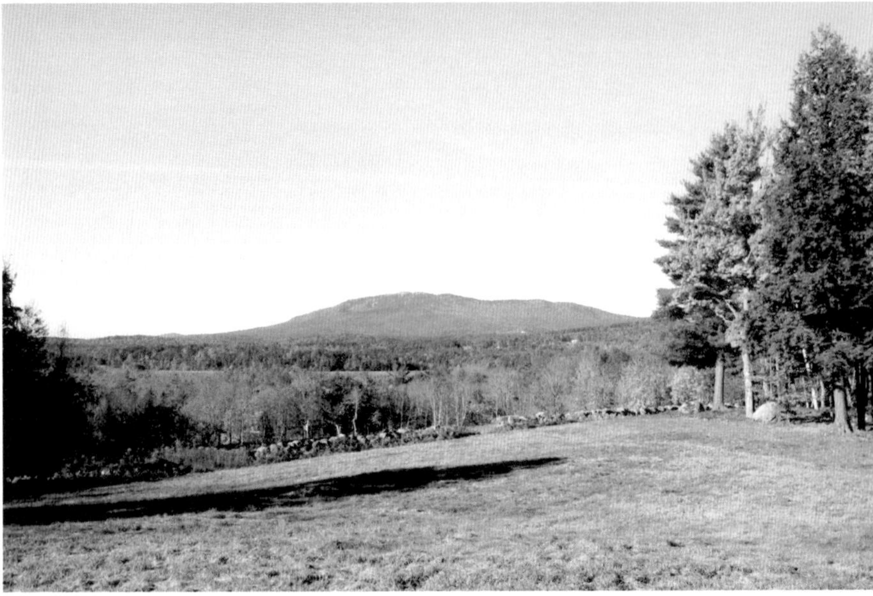

Mount Monadnock, framed by a stone wall and sugar maples from the Dublin side. *Courtesy Baxter Harris, Smiling Dog Productions.*

Ralph Waldo Emerson, Rudyard Kipling, Henry David Thoreau and the boxing champion John L. Sullivan, like thousands of hikers, climbed to the summit of Mount Monadnock, viewing all six of the New England states.

According to scuttlebutt, German spies were sending wartime information via blinking lights to u-boats lurking with raised periscopes at night just outside Boston Harbor.

Dublin, originally known as North Monadnock or Monadnock #3, was first settled by Henry Strongman from Peterborough in 1749, followed by other settlers from Sherlon, Massachusetts. Incorporated in 1771 by Governor Wentworth, it was named Dublin in honor of Strongman's birthplace in Ireland.

Mark Twain, Amy Lowell, Henry David Thoreau and Ralph Waldo Emerson were writers who felt the lure of Monadnock and the peaceful country setting, spending summers in Dublin and bringing an interest in culture. Does the Grand Lady Mount Monadnock possess some mystic power that attracts artisans to the Monadnock region?

In later years, wealthy residents of Boston and its suburbs built summer homes, not cottages, along the shore of Dublin Lake and environs.

Yankee Magazine, New England's travel magazine, and the *Old Farmers Almanac* are published in Dublin.

Greenfield is Peterborough's Monadnock neighbor to the west and was originally known as Lyndeborough addition, settled in 1753 by the Lynde family.

Today, Greenfield is best known for the Crotched Mountain Rehabilitation Center. Founded in 1953, this center treats all types of neurological disabilities and brain injuries in both children and adults.

Peterborough and neighboring villages of the Monadnock region have common bonds. They were settled at about the same period in U.S. history, and with the exception of Wilton, Dublin and Milford, they share the Contoocook River and the town meeting form of government.

Milford, on the eastern end of the Monadnock region, was incorporated in 1794 and was settled as a mill town situated on the banks of the Souhegan River. Gristmills, lumber mills and a tannery were major industries. Originally, Milford was known as Mill Ford Village. The town hall is famous for having an original Paul Revere bell, number fifty-six, in the clock tower. That bell was cast in 1802.

Originally, Hancock was within Peterborough's boundaries. Settled in 1764, Hancock was incorporated in 1779 after being set off from Peterborough and named to honor John Hancock.

Lilla Cabot Perry, noted impressionist artist, called Hancock home. Her art pieces won critical acclaim and are exhibited in major museums in the United States and Europe. Of equal importance are still-life paintings done while living in Hancock.

Native son Hayden Pearson wrote periodicals for noted newspapers and authored several books recounting rural life in Hancock during the early 1900s.

Ambassador Joseph C. Grew, career Foreign Service diplomat in the State Department, called Hancock home upon retirement. As early as January 1941, Ambassador Grew warned Washington that Japan planned to bomb Pearl Harbor. For whatever reason, this warning went unheeded.

The origin of Hancock Old Home Days dates to 1879, when the Symonds Reunion and Hancock Town Picnic were held annually in August. From thence, Hancock Old Home Days evolved—an event to reunite former residents for a nostalgic get-together. Each year, more and more attractions were added as a rededication to Hancock family and community values and traditions of years ago. The third weekend in August is an event that

Hancock citizens past and present look forward to. As teenagers, one of our hangouts was Hancock's Village Barn, a combination produce market, soda fountain and luncheonette managed by Mr. and Mrs. Joe Guinn; daughters Peggy, Cathy and Ginny; and son Dick.

Town Meeting

Another unique feature of Monadnock region towns is their form of government: the town meeting.

The ten counties in New Hampshire have no legislative function. The province of counties is administrative in nature. Each town governs itself and provides for internal needs. Counties provide law enforcement, highway maintenance and social services.

Town governance has presided ever since towns were settled and incorporated. The exceptions are the twelve municipalities designated as cities that are governed by the mayor and town council, with administrative duties delegated to the city manager.

On the second Tuesday in March, a town meeting, the foundation of local government, is held. Town residents can voice their opinions in open discussion—democracy in its purest form. To prevent chaos, there are specific ground rules. Items for discussion are outlined as "articles in the town warrant," written statements by the petitioner prior to town meeting day.

Town meeting is called to order by the standing town clerk, at which time a moderator is nominated and voted on for a two-year term. The moderator must be knowledgeable regarding local issues, have a complete grasp of parliamentary procedure, keep the meeting under control, have a sense of fairness and keep the agenda moving forward. Lincoln Lounsbury is the sole moderator I can recall. His credentials were impeccable, serving the citizens of Peterborough with distinction. Upon installation of the moderator, the order of town business proceeds. Voters elect a three-person board of selectmen/women; a town clerk; the second most important town official, a town treasurer; a trustee of funds; and a fence viewer. Police, the highway and necessary ordinances for the safety and welfare of the citizens are voted on. The board of selectmen manages decisions regarding day-to-day operations of the town. It cannot by law, make an appropriation, levy a tax or adopt laws or ordinances. These items are voted on by citizens during town meeting.

The town clerk keeps records, issues licenses and permits, is the register of deeds and collects taxes. The town clerks whom I remember were Mr. Algie Holt from March 1923 to March 1950, and Mrs. Stella Sumner, who was elected upon Mr. Holt's retirement.

The main substance of town meeting is discussion and voting on the "articles in the town warrant." A recipe for chaos? Hardly, for town meetings have governed New Hampshire towns and villages for over two hundred years.

The town school meeting is held in conjunction with town meeting. Board members are elected, and a school budget is voted on.

Back in the era that I remember, from 1937 to 1950, town meetings were well attended, all seats in the upper town hall occupied by interested, and in some years concerned, citizens of Peterborough. A member of the New Hampshire House of Representatives is also elected at town meeting. The office of fence viewer is a relic from years gone by when this official settled boundary disputes. He was also responsible for building and maintaining fences along town roads, with a crew of townspeople to assist him. Nowadays, this town official is more traditional than functional.

Traditionally, ladies from each of the churches took turns hosting a noon dinner in the lower town hall. This was an excellent fundraiser; there was a ready-to-order clientele.

Unfortunately, a number of people were stricken with food poisoning one year. Local pundits and wags had a field day—this was grist for their mill.

The History of Peterborough

Early land prospectors traveling from frontier settlements in Massachusetts before 1739 climbed to the summit of Pack Monadnock and gazed westward. Below, they beheld a panoramic valley where a forest of abundant hardwoods and softwoods grew in a fertile river valley. In a very few years, Scotch-Irish settlers from Londonderry, Lunenburg and other towns in Massachusetts would arrive, build homes, clear land and raise families, crops and livestock. Peterborough would become an established, vibrant, thriving and industrious community of both village and rural citizens.

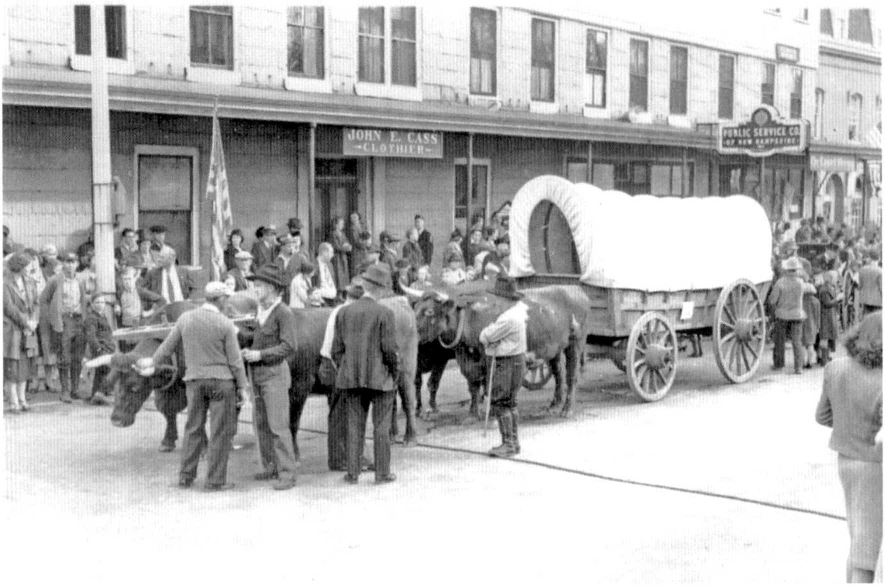

A stagecoach and oxen team with local folks dressed in period clothing during the Peterborough Bicentennial. *Collection of the Peterborough Historical Society.*

Records show that the first sale of land in what would become Peterborough occurred on November 14, 1739, when proprietor Peter Prescott deeded land to William Scott. This farmland was located on what is now the intersection of Cheney Avenue and Pine Street. This deed doesn't mean that Mr. Scott was the first settler because many parcels of land were settled long before they were deeded. In some cases, years came and went before deeds were recorded. Records show that one deed was recorded twenty-seven years after it was signed. However, 1739 establishes the origin of Peterborough, and in the fall of 1939, we attended the town's bicentennial celebration.

Covered wagons, drawn by teams of oxen, were driven by men wearing the work clothes of early settlers. Inside, there were kids and women dressed in period costumes. This is what I remember most about the bicentennial, wishing I could be in one of those covered wagons.

The year 1749 is when Peterborough was actually settled by the Scotch-Irish, who came and stayed to establish a viable community. Peterborough was legally incorporated in 1760, signifying that all pertinent affairs of the town were transferred from the proprietors to the citizens of the town. From

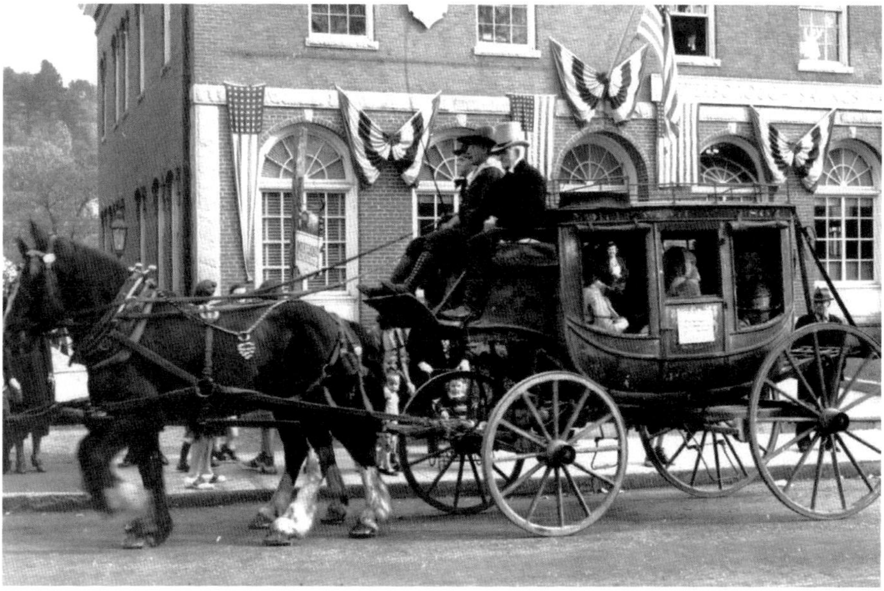

A stagecoach and team of horses with local folks dressed in period clothing during the Peterborough Bicentennial. *Collection of the Peterborough Historical Society.*

this date until the present, all town meeting proceedings were duly recorded by the town clerk. Apparently, one of the qualifications of a town clerk was neat, legible handwriting because all the town meeting proceedings are clearly readable. We know exactly how voters acted on matters of town business, referred to as "articles of the town warrant."

After 1760, what had been referred to as a settlement was now a bona fide town, to be known as Peterborough. Day-to-day business affairs, town operations and implementing the "articles of the town warrant" came under the jurisdiction of the board of selectmen.

How did the incorporated town of Peterborough come by its name? One theory reasons that it was because Peter Prescott was the original proprietor. A proprietor is an individual (or group of men) who has been granted certain tracts of land by the king of England. His function is similar to that of a feudal lord: to pass laws and decrees, assess taxes, establish schools and churches and maintain roads. He would also sell or rent acreage to individuals and be responsible for public affairs until a town became incorporated. Upon incorporation, the town would be governed and managed by a board of selectmen elected at the annual town meeting.

When we first arrived in town from Ames, Iowa, in 1937, the folklore we heard was that a hermit named Peter, who was the original settler in 1739, had lived in a cave near what is now Cheney Avenue. According to historians, that tale is strictly a fable and has no basis in fact. It did, however, make for an interesting story. Historians have agreed that most likely the town derived its name from Charles Mordaunt, the Third Earl of Peterborough, England, a hero during the War of Spanish Succession.

Two illustrious and courageous war heroes were Peterborough native sons. Brigadier General James Miller fought in the War of 1812 and was awarded the Congressional Gold Medal, the nation's highest award for valor. Miller State Park, the oldest state park in New Hampshire, was named in his honor. Brigadier General Miller was born in Peterborough in 1776 and died in Temple, New Hampshire, in 1858. Pack Monadnock is located in Miller State Park and is within sight of Temple.

Isaac D. White, known to family and friends as Davis, was born in Peterborough on March 6, 1901. His father owned and operated White's Machine Shop on Nubanusitt Lane. In 1922, Davis graduated from Norwich University, where he was enrolled in the ROTC program. He was commissioned as second lieutenant in the U.S. Army, Cavalry. He assisted in organizing what would become the Second Armored Division, holding all ranks from major to major general and division commanding officer. Major General White fought in eight combat campaigns in North Africa, Sicily and Europe during World War II. Promoted to lieutenant general, he participated in the Korean War and was awarded the highest South Korean medal for valor. Lieutenant General White was decorated with medals from the U.S. government, as well as from several foreign allies.

A noteworthy native of Peterborough was William Diamond, a nineteen-year-old drummer boy who was guarding John Hancock's house. On April 18, 1775, after Paul Revere sounded the alarm that the British were coming, drummer Diamond played a drum roll that was a call to arms. His great-great-grandson is Arthur L. Diamond, also a native of Peterborough, who served in World War I.

Six governors of the state of New Hampshire have been born or raised in Peterborough or called the town home. Large cities nationwide would be hard put to make this claim. The governors are as follows: Jeremiah Smith, 1809–10; John S. Steele, 1844–46; Person C. Cheney, 1875–77; George A. Ramsdell, 1897–99; Robert P. Bass, 1911–13; and Walter

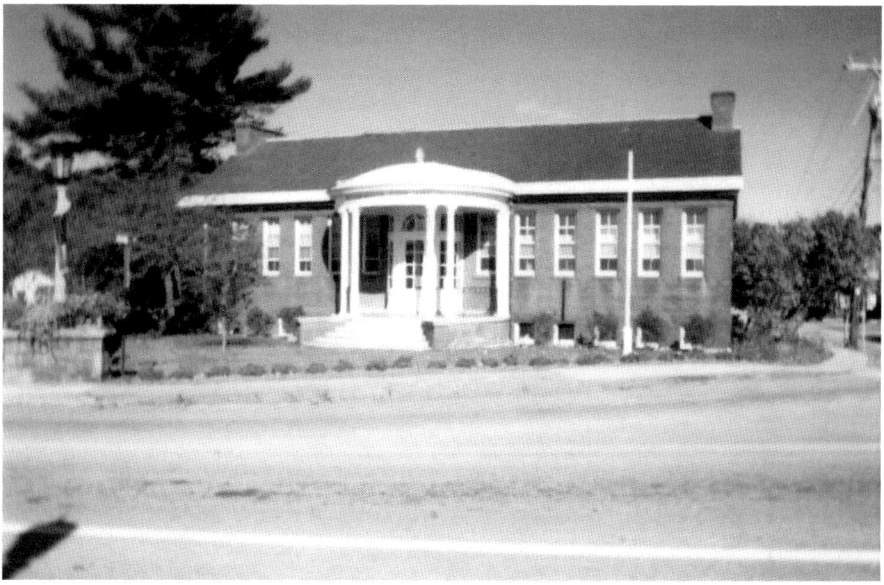

Peterborough Library, the first public, free library supported by taxation in the world.

Peterson, 1969–73. Jeremiah Smith was the brother of Robert Bass's great-grandfather.

Peterborough statesmen have held office at both the state and federal levels. Perkins Bass, son of Robert P. Bass, was a member of the New Hampshire House of Representatives from 1939 to 1941, and again from 1947 to 1949, and a member of the Senate from 1949 to 1951. He was elected to the New Hampshire House of Representatives again in 1955 and served until 1963. Charles Bass, son of Perkins, presently serves in the U.S. House of Representatives.

Town meeting day in 1833 was April 9. A resolution was adopted that created "a free, publicly owned library, supported by local taxation." This was the first library of its kind, under those conditions, in the world. The rationale was that a library is, in fact, a form of education for adults as well as school-age students. There were four articles of the town warrant related to the free library issue. No doubt, there were adults living in Peterborough who, for whatever reason, had to drop out of school when they were youngsters, so the library was their continued education.

The first library was in the basement of the town hall, shelved 3,732 books and had an annual budget of $165.30. The original building was constructed in 1893. It was deeded to the Town of Peterborough in 1926, and in 2006, it was placed on the National Register of Historic Places.

Peterborough men and women have always stepped up, answering the call to serve in the military to protect the United States. Military service dates back to the French and Indian War of 1755–56, the Revolutionary War, the War of 1812, the Mexican War, the Civil War, the Spanish-American War, World War I, World War II, the Korean War and the Vietnam War. An honor roll inscribed with the names of those who served and those who died doing so through the years is located at a memorial near the town hall on Grove Street. "All gave some. Some gave all."

Drama

Peterborough has had a role in the world of drama that goes back to 1867, when amateur thespians staged plays over the stable at the Bleak House.

Mary Ware Laughton brought a summer theater troupe to a location on the Middle Hancock Road in 1913. Later, in 1919, Mrs. Guy Currier founded the Mariarden Theater-in-the-Woods at the same location. It would become the first out-of-doors stage in America and included a school for dance and drama.

A few miles up Middle Hancock Road, Mrs. Edith Bonds Stearns purchased the Hadley Farm in 1931. Mrs. Stearns's daughter, Isabelle, aspired to a stage career, so the Stearns family wrote plays for their own entertainment using the original rustic Hadley dairy barn as a theater. It has changed little over the years.

A patron of arts and drama, Mrs. Stearns founded the Peterborough Players, the summer stock theater that we know today. It is highly regarded nationwide. From the beginning, Mrs. Stearns has elevated the criterion of theater professionalism in her choice of productions and her selection of both professional actresses and actors and those aspiring to stage careers. Raising the artistic bar high, the Peterborough Players have brought drama to the Monadnock region, staging four or five plays during the summer—eight productions of each play. They come each summer to the Peterborough Playhouse to stage classical drama at its best: *Charlie's Aunt*, *Our Town*, *The Glass Menagerie*, *On the Town*, *You Can't Take It With You* and *Teahouse of the August Moon*, to mention but a few. Thornton Wilder's Pulitzer Prize–winning play

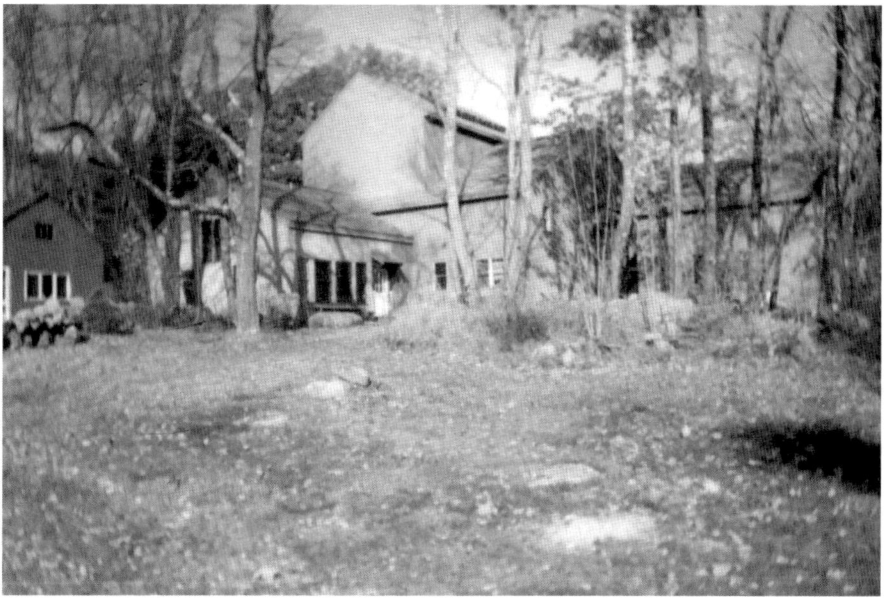

Peterborough Players summer theater on the former Hadley Farm.

Our Town has been on the playbill numerous times over the years. For one production, Mr. Fletcher Dole played Howie Newsome, the milkman. Mr. Dole was Thornton Wilder's inspiration for Howie, and having delivered Guernsey milk in glass bottles for half a century, Mr. Dole was about as professional a milkman as they come.

The number of past Peterborough Players who have gone on to Broadway and Hollywood is legend, and they are a living tribute to Mrs. Edith Bond Stearns's high standards and her dedication to drama and the stage. Three who come to mind are James Whitmore, Rosanne Cox and Robert Morse, who received rave reviews for his role in the Broadway musical *How to Succeed in Business Without Really Trying*, winning a Tony Award in 1962. James Whitmore starred in the movie *Oklahoma!*.

No doubt, the Peterborough Players will stage a production of *Our Town* sometime in the future. One of the props will be Mr. Dole's bottle carrier and six glass milk bottles, courtesy of Dotty Dole Johnson.

MacDowell Colony

Edward MacDowell was a world-renowned composer and pianist and chairman of the music department at Columbia University, and he performed with the Boston Symphony and the Philharmonic Society of New York. A man that busy certainly needed a vacation and time away from the hustle, bustle and pressures of the big city. So, he and his wife, Marian, began spending their summers in Peterborough, New Hampshire.

They were drawn to this area because of the natural beauty, peace and quiet of a rural setting. In 1896, they purchased a one-hundred-acre farm, Hillcrest, where they would spend the remainder of their lives. At Hillcrest, Edward built a log cabin in the woods, which became his studio, where he composed most of his best music. Edward and Marian asked themselves, "Why not provide similar facilities for both accomplished, as well as aspiring, artists so they can pursue their art disciplines in a peaceful, quiet and relaxed environment?" With the purchase of an adjacent three-hundred-acre farm, MacDowell Colony became a reality.

In 1907, the MacDowell Association was incorporated; its purpose was to carry out the wishes of Edward and Marian, to provide and maintain an

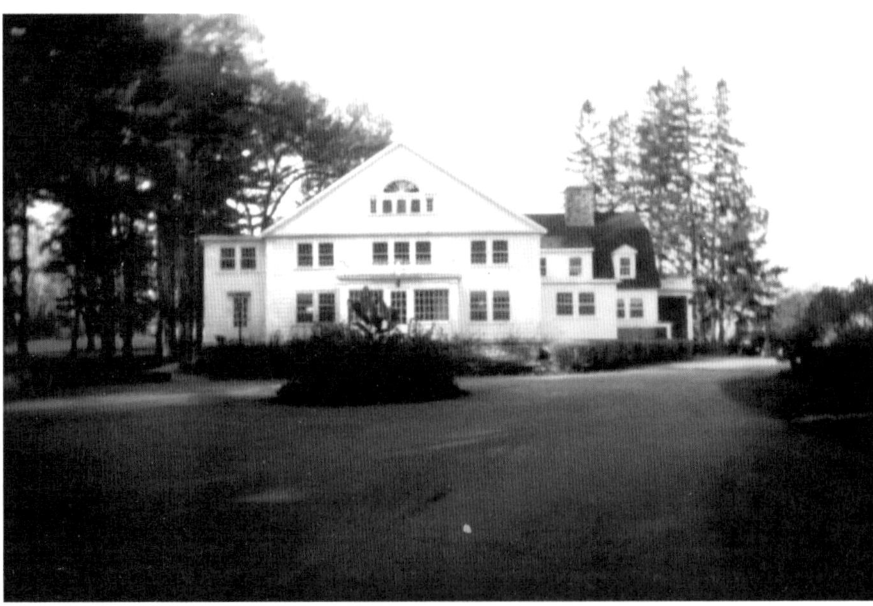

MacDowell Colony Hall. Residents dine together at evening dinner.

artistic colony as the couple had planned. Edward was in failing health, but he did live long enough to see a few artists at work at MacDowell Colony. He died in 1908 and was buried at the colony. Marian rests in an adjacent grave.

Eventually, thirty-two cabins were built throughout the wooded acreage to serve as art studios. The residents dine together in the evening at Colony Hall, while other meals are brought to their studios.

Edward MacDowell realized that artists from various disciplines living in a community "will, by association, bring new and different artistic dimensions to the lives of each member."

MacDowell Colony is unique, having hosted thousands of artists from across the United States and foreign countries since 1907. Artists, both established and aspiring, come here to excel and advance in all the art forms in a rural setting that found favor with Edward MacDowell himself. Twenty-six Pulitzer Prizes have been bestowed on MacDowell Colony alumni. Folks in Peterborough best remember Thornton Wilder, a resident at MacDowell Colony, who wrote the play *Our Town*, receiving the Pulitzer Prize in 1938. The inspiration for Grover's Corners in the play is Peterborough. As previously mentioned, Mr. Fletcher Dole was the inspiration for Howie Newsome, the milkman in the play.

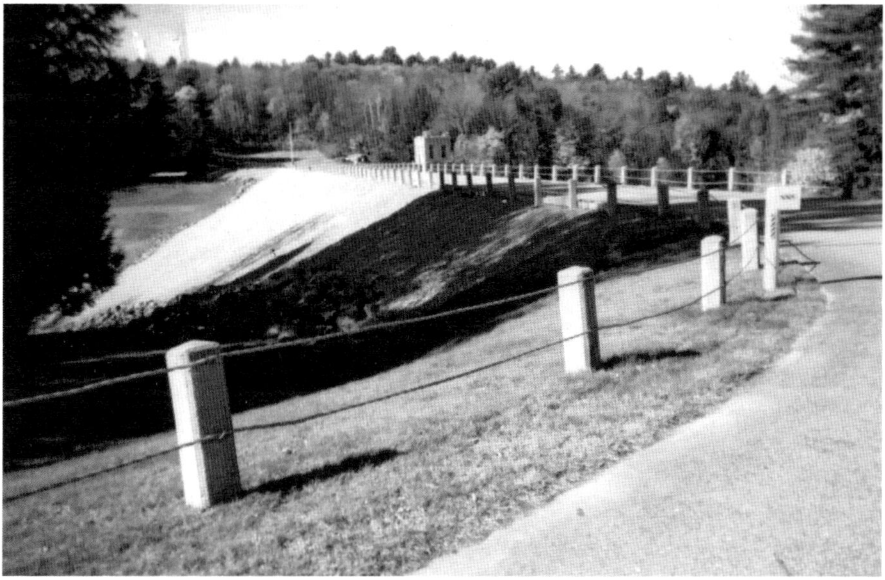

MacDowell Dam, built by the Army Corps of Engineers and dedicated in 1949.

In 1949, the U.S. Corps of Engineers designed and constructed a flood control dam above West Peterborough. With the exception of cement sluiceways, the dam was entirely earthen, with stone riprap on both sides for soil stability. In recognition of Edward MacDowell, noted classical composer and resident of Peterborough, the dam was named in his honor.

Edward MacDowell is buried in a plot on upper High Street, on the village side of Colony Hall, adjacent to the Peterborough Golf Club, for which he donated the land.

American Guernsey Cattle Club

Since 1894, Peterborough has been the home of the national headquarters of the American Guernsey Cattle Club. Previously, the main office was located in Farmington, Connecticut. From 1877 to 1894, Edward Norton was the executive secretary-treasurer. In 1894, William H. Caldwell was appointed executive secretary-treasurer, so he relocated the main office to his farm, Clover Ridge, on Old Dublin Road in Peterborough. By 1911, he employed fourteen clerks and secretaries. In the 1940s and '50s, he employed approximately 190 people at attractive salaries, contributing to the economy of Peterborough.

In the early days of the Guernsey Club at Clover Ridge, all the clerical work was done using paper, pen and ink; portable typewriters came out in 1912. All the registration certificates and milk production records were recorded by hand.

The clerks and secretaries, young ladies who lived in the village, drove to work by horse and buggy or sleigh across Evans' Flats to Clover Ridge Farm.

One of the original employees was Miss Etta M. Smith, an accountant and our next-door neighbor on High Street. She also wrote *History of Peterborough—A Genealogy*, Book Two.

The office outgrew the facilities at Clover Ridge, so it was moved to a large residence at the corner of Grove and School Streets.

The national headquarters was growing by leaps and bounds so that by 1918, a brick structure was built on the same site to accommodate more office space. In 1919, two additions were added at a cost of $65,000—$9,000

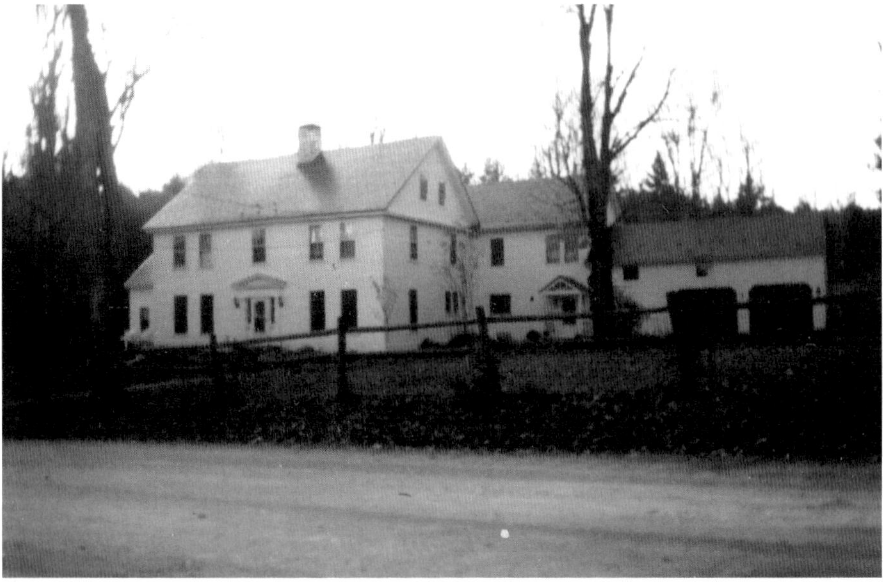

Original headquarters of the American Guernsey Cattle Club at Clover Ridge Farm.

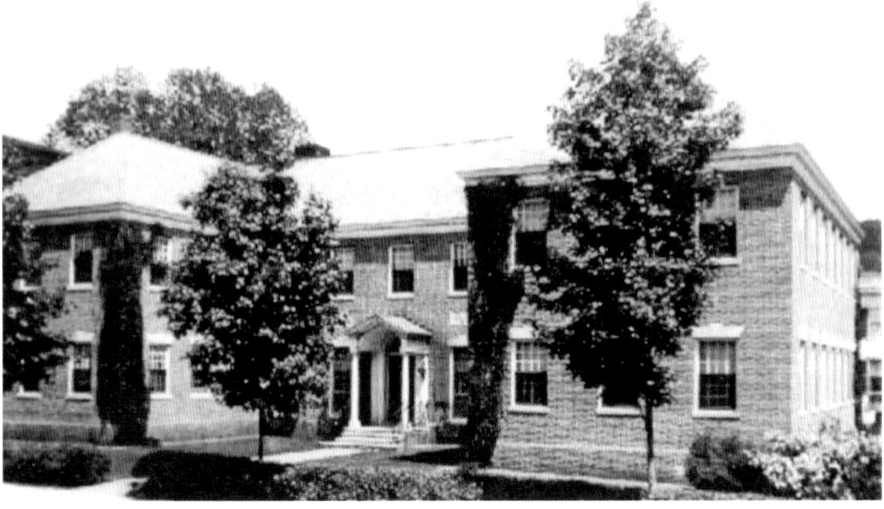

Present headquarters of the American Guernsey Cattle Club. *Collection of the Peterborough Historical Society.*

under the estimate. That structure, a middle section with two wings, stands at the corner of Grove and School Streets today.

In 1922, Karl B. Musser was appointed executive secretary-treasurer and, by virtue of his leadership, would chart the course of growth and development of the American Guernsey Cattle Club for the next thirty-two years. The club is a tribute to the dedication of three men—Edward Norton, William H. Caldwell and Karl B. Musser—whose stewardship spanned seventy-seven years.

By 1937, membership in the Guernsey Club had increased, and more and more animals were being registered and enrolled in production and classification programs. These numbers meant that more office space was needed, so additional facilities were rented in three different buildings, which proved to be unwieldy, at best.

Something had to be done regarding additional office space, so a larger building on upper Main Street was constructed in 1950.

The role of the American Guernsey Cattle Club is manifold; it was organized to serve its members, who have registered purebred Guernsey cattle. Each animal has a Certificate of Registry, inscribed with its purebred name, ID number, date of birth, owner, breeder (and his or her address), sire, dam and a sketch of color markings to establish identity. The definition of a purebred is "an animal, male or female, which can be traced, in unbroken lineage, to the cradle of the breed; in this case, the Isle of Guernsey, in the English Channel." That's the importance of having one national clearinghouse that issues registration certificates.

Promotion

Promoting the Guernsey cow and Guernsey milk is another function of the American Guernsey Cattle Club. At the 1893 World's Columbia Exposition, held in Chicago, Guernsey milk—yellow in color and flavorful—was advertised, promoted and well received. Back then, milk was sold in glass bottles, which today are a collector's item. This World's Fair, the grandest of them all, ran from May 15, when it was opened by President Grover Cleveland, to October 30, when it closed after being viewed by twenty-seven million people.

In September 1923, the trademark "Golden Guernsey Products" was registered with the U.S. Patent Office. From that day forward, the Golden

Guernsey Division of the Guernsey Club has been responsible for the success of marketing Guernsey milk for the benefit of Guernsey breeders and Golden Guernsey distributors.

Promoting the Guernsey breed has been a success story from the beginning. In 1928, a University of Wisconsin graduate, E.W. "Al" Bunce, was hired to head the Promotion Division. An innovative promoter, he had no peers. During his career, he carried off some impressive promotion activities.

One of his most unusual and impressive promotion stunts was sending three Guernsey cows with Admiral Richard E. Byrd to Antarctica in 1933. They provided milk for the entire expedition crew, and when Admiral Byrd became sick, he claimed, "The milk from those Guernseys pulled me out of my tailspin!" Just the logistics of feeding and caring for cows in such a hostile environment is mind-boggling. A movie film was produced, *Guernseys Discover Antarctica*, and when the three cows returned to the United States in 1934, they were wined and dined like royalty in Washington, D.C., New York City and Boston. While in Antarctica, one of the cows had a bull calf, which was named Ice Berg. There hasn't been a dairy cattle promotion scheme that got that much news coverage and publicity before or since.

Guernseys Fly

On June 10, 1946, ten Guernsey heifers were flown from Teterboro, New Jersey, to Bogotá, Columbia, in a DC3 cargo plane. Senor Antonio Pradilla instructed my dad to select some Guernsey breeding stock for his dairy farm. Shipping cattle by boat presented some real problems, so Dad decided to try the airways. This was a first for any dairy cattle and created considerable media attention. Two hundred news reporters and three newsreel crews covered the event. The flight took seventeen and a half hours, with two stopovers, and upon their arrival, Senor Pradilla wired back, "Heifers landed yesterday in wonderful condition, found an excellent lot selected." Dad related, "This was one of the best wires I've ever received." The media coverage was tremendous all over the world, with unusual newspaper headlines: "Beef Flies High" or "Price of Beef Goes Up." News reporters didn't realize that these were dairy, not beef, animals! A more acceptable headline stated, "Guernseys Fly High."

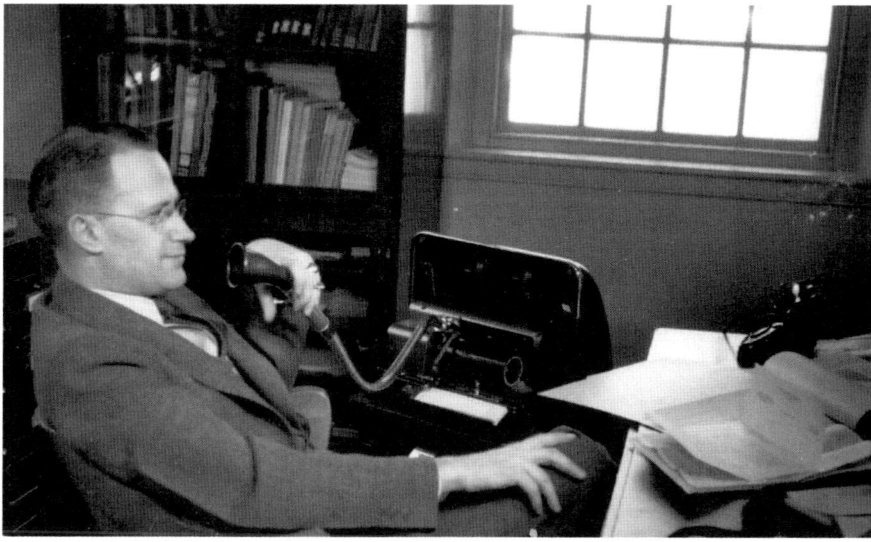

Earl Shultz at work for the American Guernsey Cattle Club, dictating a letter on a Dictaphone.

Guernsey Breeders' Journal

This publication had its origin in 1885, when a sixteen-page magazine was printed and sent to all members of the Guernsey Club. It included news items and details of meetings and shows and listed registration transfers. In 1910, the *Journal*, as we know it today, printed its first edition. It expanded on the original by including production records, breeder advertisements and reports of consignment and dispersal sales. Back then, the editors I remember were Lincoln Lounsbury and Richard Price, both of whom were masters of dairy breed journalism.

Field Representatives (Extension)

Keeping members of the Guernsey Club connected to the home office and giving them a sense of belonging is an important responsibility. The Guernsey Club had a national extension staff, whose duties were to help Guernsey breeders with registrations and transfers; assist in organizing field days, shows and sales; and keep breeders informed in regard to Guernsey breed goals and policy. My dad was hired by the Guernsey Club in November

1937 as a field representative, with New England, Ohio, New York, Pennsylvania, New Jersey, Delaware and West Virginia as his territory. State Guernsey Associations in Massachusetts, New York, Ohio, Pennsylvania and New Jersey also had state field men who worked in cooperation with the national field staff.

Executive secretary-treasurer Karl Musser was a strong advocate of the value of an effective extension program. During the Great Depression of the 1930s, he did not cut field staff to economize—and it paid off, because during the Depression, the decline in membership was less than that of other dairy breed organizations.

Performance Register

At the 1941 annual meeting of the Guernsey Club, it was voted to compile a *Performance Register* comprising a volume for bulls and one for cows. These publications would contain progeny and milk production records so that Guernsey breeders could look up information on any given bull or cow. The *Performance Register* division at the home office records milk production figures for cows on the Advanced Register program. From 1901 to 1947, 112,358 production figures were recorded. Since the Guernsey Club was organized, over 428,000 males and over 1 million females have been registered.

Herd Register

The primary purpose of the America Guernsey Cattle Club—and its reason for being—is to record and provide certificates of registration for eligible Guernsey animals. When animals are sold or there is a change in ownership, the Guernsey Club attaches a transfer of ownership to the original registration paper; a duplicate is on file in the home office.

To be eligible for registration, a Guernsey must trace his or her beginning in unbroken lineage to the Isle of Guernsey.

A registration certificate catalogues the following information: registered name and number, date of birth, sire and dam (and their birth dates and registration numbers), the owner and breeder (and their addresses) and a sketch of the animal for identification. When the animal is classified, the score is stamped on the registration paper. Integrity of the individual breeder is paramount to maintaining a system whereby each animal registered is, in fact, purebred.

Brief History of the Breed

In AD 960, Robert of Normandy sent a group of militant monks to the Isle of Guernsey, located in the English Channel. The monks were militant because pirates had been harassing the local citizenry. The monks brought with them native cattle from Normandy and Brittany, France. Cattle were an ideal choice of livestock because they could graze the lush pastures to produce milk and cream. From the milk, the monks made a delicious brand of cheese, and the cream was churned to make butter. Whey was fed to the bull calves to produce veal. As an end product, cow manure was used to grow an abundance of vegetables. Apparently, the monks were good cattle judges because they selected the better individuals, crossbreeding them and eating the rest. Over a period of time, they developed what became known as Guernseys.

To ensure a pure strain of Guernseys, measures were taken in 1789 against importing cattle to the Isle of Guernsey. In 1824, stringent laws prohibited the importation of dairy cattle, resulting in a closed herd.

Some of the bulls were altered, becoming oxen, which the monks used as beasts of burden to till the soil. A Guernsey ox would weigh fifteen hundred pounds, was docile and could work in the yoke or between shafts to pull a wagon.

Guernseys were first imported to the United States in 1831 from the Isle of Guernsey and shipped to Cow Island, located on Lake Winnipesaukee, New Hampshire. In 1935, the New Hampshire legislature renamed it Guernsey Island. A large number of Guernseys were imported to the United States in the early 1920s, after which the number of imported animals dwindled and finally ceased. By that time, Guernsey breeders were developing American bloodlines.

George A. Morison, author of *History of Peterborough, New Hampshire*, Book One, states, "Peterborough should always recognize the great benefit which it has received from its association with the Guernsey Cattle Club and from the fine group of public-spirited citizens which it has brought here as employees to become citizens of our town."

New England Hurricane of 1938

On September 21, 1938, a hurricane slammed into Peterborough, New Hampshire, with full force and shrieking winds. In theory, hurricanes lose their ferocity after heading inland, but you couldn't tell that to residents of Peterborough on that fateful day. To make matters worse, the region was deluged with a torrential rainfall that caused catastrophic flooding in the village. If this weren't adversity enough, the Peterborough Transcript Printing Company and the Walbridge & Taylor feed mill caught fire. Both buildings were situated on the bank of the Contoocook River, which flooded Depot Square and lower Main Street. To worsen matters, the Nubanusit River, also at flood stage, emptied into the Contoocook River above Depot Square. This was a bad situation for the Peterborough Volunteer Fire Department because both blazing buildings were surrounded by water, so they couldn't fight the conflagration. Buildings from Depot Square to Main Street were all destroyed.

The origin of the '38 hurricane was a West Indian cyclone that had been moving rapidly on a northeasterly course for four days. It was hoped that this hurricane would move eastward and out to the Atlantic, but that, unfortunately, was not the case. It came up past Cape Hatteras, North Carolina, slamming into the U.S. mainland from South Jersey to Boston, Massachusetts.

Back then, high-tech warning systems—such as using radar, Doppler and satellites to track the path, strength and speed of hurricanes—hadn't been developed. The storms were known as cyclones rather than hurricanes and

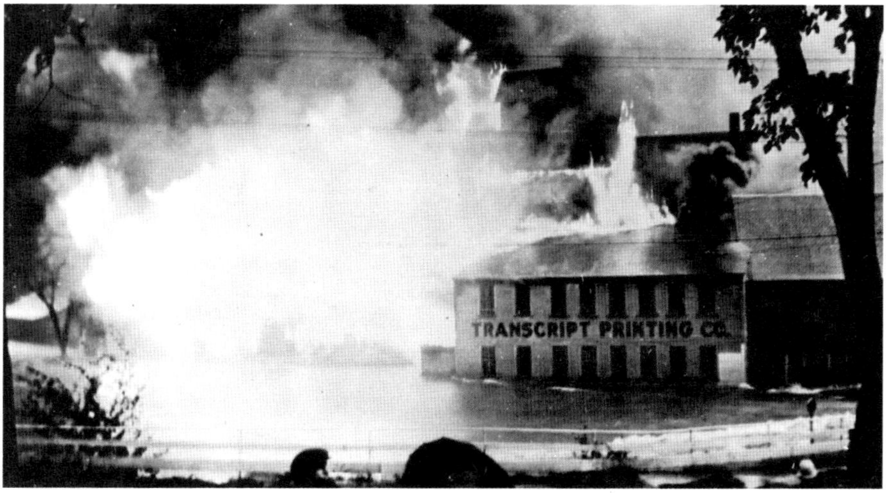

Fire damage due to the 1938 hurricane. *Collection of the Peterborough Historical Society.*

were tracked by ships in the Caribbean, which reported them to weather stations in Washington, D.C.; San Juan, Puerto Rico; and Havana, Cuba.

The '38 hurricane was a different type of monster. There had never been a cyclone of that magnitude in that part of the globe before, and it traveled at such a high rate of speed—six hundred miles in only twelve hours. In the early stages, most thought the wind and rain was the traditional "line storm" that occurs when the sun crosses the equator in September.

With power and telephone lines down, it was impossible for a warning system to function, and what information that did get through was in bits and pieces, causing confusion. Communication systems weren't nearly as advanced in 1938 as they are today. Keep in mind that this hurricane was traveling at fifty miles per hour!

The term "hurricane" is derived from the vocabulary of an extinct aboriginal Indian tribe of the West Indies describing a cyclone.

In terms of magnitude, the 1900 Galveston, Texas hurricane killed between 8,000 and 12,000 people. The 1889 Johnstown, Pennsylvania flood was a horrendous disaster in the United States, claiming over 3,000 lives and causing millions of dollars' worth of property damage. The second worst natural disaster would be the 1938 New England hurricane, which claimed 680 people killed and caused $400 million worth of property damage.

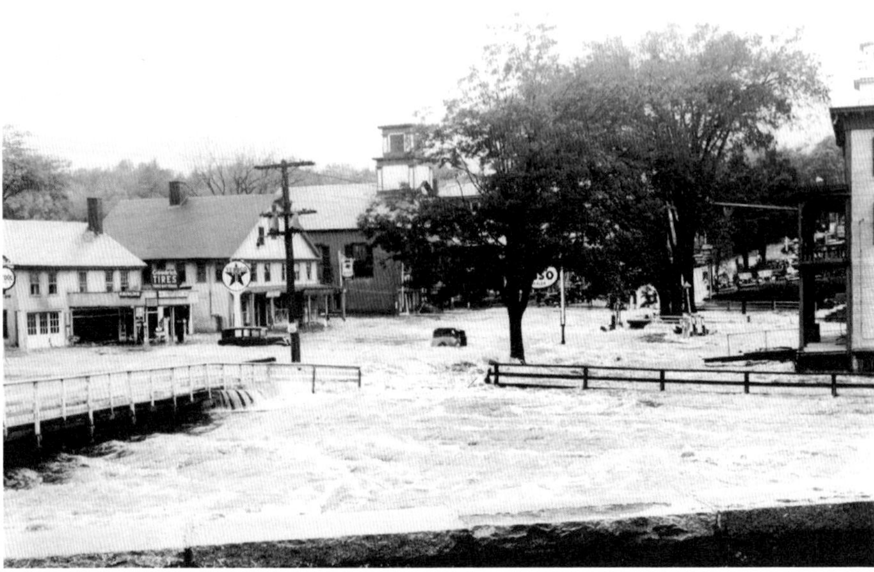

Flood damage due to the 1938 hurricane. *Collection of the Peterborough Historical Society.*

Prior to the hurricane, several days' worth of rain had loosened the soil around the shallow root system of white pines, making them easy prey to violent winds; they went down like a pile of jack sticks.

None of the sugar maples around our house or in the neighborhood had blown down, but the virgin stand of white pines at the golf club was leveled, lying on the ground like so many jackstraws. MacDowell Colony lost most of the pine tree stands on its four hundred acres of woodland.

In the early afternoon of September 21, the rain let up, so my mom decided to walk downtown to see what was going on. She recalls how still and eerie the air was—not a breeze stirring. That situation didn't last long because, out of nowhere, the full fury of hurricane winds hit with a vengeance and lasted for twelve hours. Mom relates how she literally crawled on her hands and knees up Main Street and then up High Street, going from tree to tree and telephone pole to telephone pole to keep from being blown away.

Hurricane-force winds blew down trees, so we were without electricity and phone service for a couple of weeks. School was cancelled for the time being. Unfortunately, the weather turned cold, so we used a kerosene stove

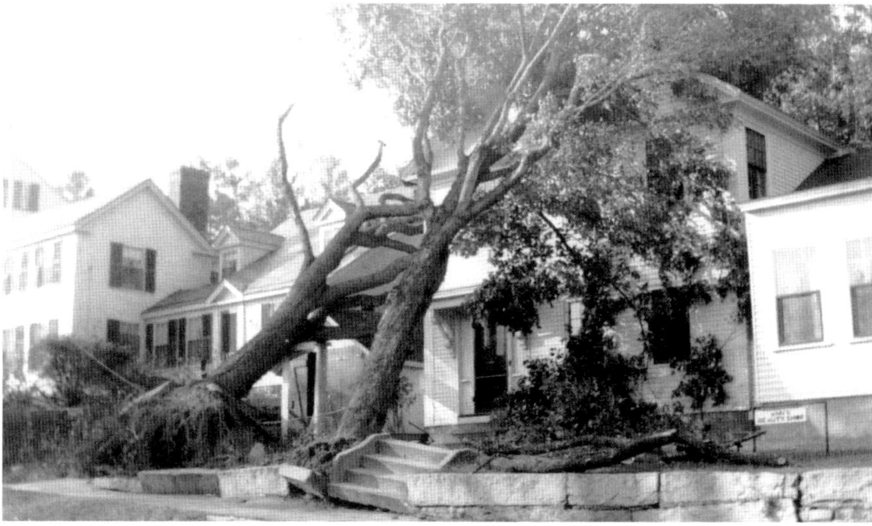

More flood damage due to the 1938 hurricane. *Collection of the Peterborough Historical Society.*

for heat and cooking. Candles and kerosene lamps gave us light; one of the lamps was a wedding present to Grandpa and Grandma Kennedy.

"Hovering in Colony Hall as the hurricane raged outside, we could see magnificent hundred-year-old white pines begin to topple," recalls Dotty Dole, who was working at the MacDowell Colony to earn money to attend Bates College. "We couldn't get home because fallen trees and downed power lines blocked the road. In the evening, we saw the red glow of fire as it consumed downtown Peterborough. It was scary!"

Mr. Dole was janitor at the Congregational church, and because the floodwaters were rising, he thought it necessary to do what he could to protect the church furnaces.

"Dad had saddled Charlie and rode him across the bridge spanning the Contoocook River in front of the library," Dotty recollects. "He was the last person across and had to return home by way of North Peterborough via the Hunt Road, thence to Upper High Street and home."

Fortunately, no homes were destroyed or permanently damaged in Peterborough, although some houses were flooded. Roads were washed out, electric and phone lines downed and millions upon millions of board feet of virgin white pine blown down.

Salvaging the hurricane timber began that fall and was fully underway by the early spring of 1939. In some localities, lumber camps were established in the woods, complete with a bunkhouse, camp kitchen, mess hall and sawmill. In other situations, logs were transported by truck to existing sawmills.

Back then, horses and teamsters were used to snake out logs because mechanical log skidders were unheard-of. Lumberjacks wielding double-bitted axes and two-man crosscut saws trimmed logs and cut them to length. This was before one-man chainsaws were commonplace.

Actually, Andreas Stihl (pronounced "steel"), a German mechanical engineer, did invent a gasoline-powered chainsaw in 1929, which he patented. It is possible that lumberjacks did have chainsaws back then, but I don't recall them being used. Seventy-seven years after this invention, Stihl chainsaws are highly regarded and have been used extensively in timber harvesting worldwide.

A teamster and his team of rugged workhorses would snake logs, one by one, to a skid way, where lumberjacks, using peaveys (also called cant dogs), loaded them onto a log scoot. A scoot is basically a heavy-duty sled with steel-edged, four- by eight-inch runners that are connected by four-by-four crossbeams. Pulled by a team, they transport logs out of the woods to a roadside skid way, where they are loaded on trucks and then transported to a sawmill.

The Murray brothers were teamsters working in the woods with their horses and doing custom plowing and soil fitting in the spring.

On upper High Street, a large stand of virgin white pines on the edge of the Peterborough Golf Club went down during the hurricane. The Murray brothers and their teams of horses logged this section of woods, bringing the logs on scoots up to the roadside.

Civilian Conservation Corp (CCC) recruits performed a valuable service in helping to clean up the hurricane aftermath. There were thirteen CCC camps throughout the state, housing approximately 450 recruits per camp. Other work projects included tree planting, park development and tree disease control.

Prior to the 1938 New England hurricane, white-tailed deer were scarce in southern New Hampshire, but during the post-hurricane years, the deer herd saw a tremendous increase in numbers due to a change in its environmental habitat. When the virgin white pine plantations were destroyed, the new growth that took over provided an abundance of browse for the increasing numbers of deer, which kept multiplying by leaps and bounds. Though most of the downed trees were logged, treetops, limbs and scattered blow-down provided cover and a haven for white-tailed deer.

A beneficial offshoot of the 1938 New England hurricane was the abundance of sawdust available to dairy farmers for cow bedding. Some of these old sawdust piles remained for many years after the hurricane, and sawmill operators were only too glad to have farmers cart it away at no cost. In the late summer, Mr. Dole would drive Charlie, his Morgan gelding workhorse hooked to the wagon, down to a sawmill at North Peterborough. Using wooden rakes turned upside down, we made long twin rows of dry sawdust, which we scooped up with a shovel and put into big citrus-pulp burlap bags. Charlie then drew them home for next winter's bedding for the cows. The sawdust we bagged up came from an old pile that had been sun dried for a year or two; Mr. Dole didn't want green sawdust to bed his cattle. He must have been ahead of his time because dairy cattle specialists in the twenty-first century discovered mastitis-causing pathogens in green sawdust.

Those who remember in vivid detail the catastrophic aftermath of the '38 hurricane—and they are dwindling in number—will all agree to a person that it was the worst disaster they can remember. Peterborough and southern New Hampshire have had their share of nor'easter blizzards and sub-zero winter temperatures. These, a person can handle, but there's no way to deal with a hurricane except to hunker down and pray for the best.

The Dole Family

Dole Homestead

At the crest of a lawn that slopes toward High Street stands the Dole homestead, a Colonial-style farmhouse whose red bricks have become faded by the winds, winters and sun of a couple hundred years. Old, gnarled and majestic maples stand guard along both sides of the circular driveway, which has seen stagecoaches arriving and then leaving on their journeys to distant towns. The visual evidence indicates that at one time the house where Mr. and Mrs. Dole lived for nearly sixty years and raised four daughters was a stagecoach inn. At the rear of the house is an ell that was a kitchen, and adjacent was a room where the stage passengers rested and had something to eat while they waited for the next coach to depart. Passengers arrived and departed through a door on the west side of the waiting room.

To the rear of the house stands a barn, weathered by time and the New Hampshire elements, where the stagecoach teams were housed. The barn has both a front and back door so that arriving stages could change teams and then depart through the back door and down the circular drive to High Street. However, there is a granite hitching post where the teams could be changed during pleasant weather.

Use your imagination and you can hear the jangle of trace chains on the doubletree. They trot a little faster up the drive because they know their work is done for the day and that another team will continue the journey. They will be rewarded with a bait of oats, a pail of water, a forkful of

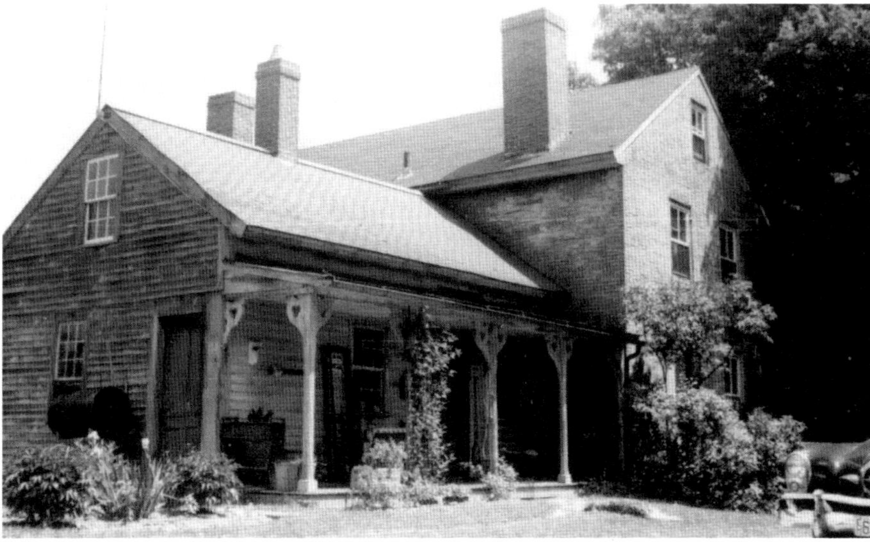

Dole Homestead, originally a stagecoach station. *Courtesy of Dotty Dole Johnson.*

timothy hay and a straw-bedded stall for the night. When the snowfall is heavy and during the muddy season in early spring, two teams will be hitched to the stage.

Mrs. Dole was an ardent gardener, and any flower, shrub or bush she planted grew and flourished. Both annual and perennial flowers grew and blossomed in a large bed just beyond the waiting room, which in later years was a summer kitchen. The drive leading to the house and barn was constructed using coal ashes that over time had packed hard and gave Charlie traction when he pulled full loads of hay to the barn.

When the Doles arrived at their new home in 1922 at 34 High Street, the barn had stalls on both sides for the stagecoach horses. Stalls on the west side were converted to cow beds for his four purebred Guernsey cows.

As mentioned earlier, the barn had doors in both ends. The front one was a sliding door, and the rear one was on hinges, which was almost the undoing of the barn years ago. During the 1938 hurricane, the rear door blew open, and after a struggle against the raging winds, Mr. Dole finally got it closed. Using planks, he nailed it shut permanently, where it remains to this day.

Their large vegetable garden was located across the street on the edge of a small hayfield. Included in the garden were several rows of gladiolus in every

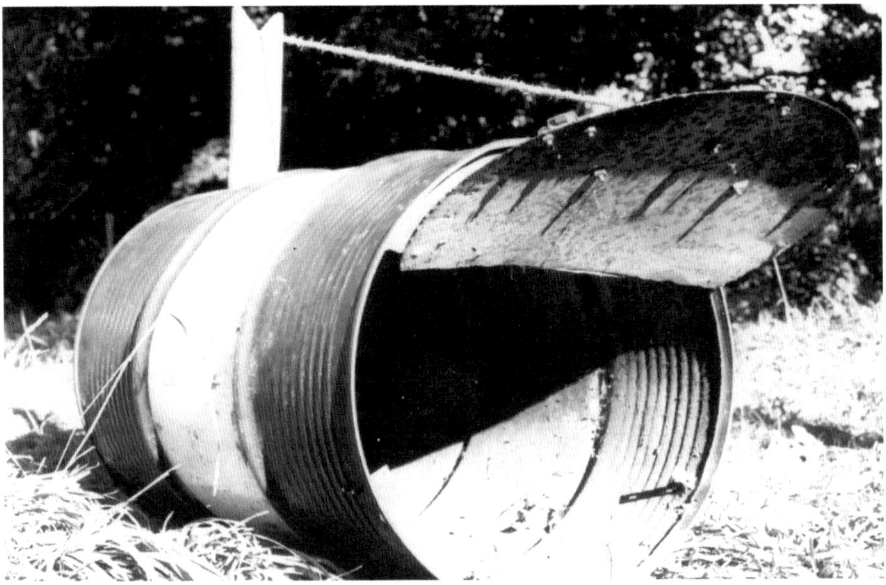

Mr. Dole's raccoon trap. *Courtesy of Dotty Dole Johnson.*

color you could imagine, some even multicolored. They came into bloom about the third week of August, so Mrs. Dole took several baskets to decorate the pulpit of the Congregational church each Sunday until the first frost in the fall, when they were dug up, dried out and planted the next spring.

Each spring, Mrs. Dole planted multicolored morning glories that climbed up strings from ground level to the eaves on the back piazza, creating gorgeous festoons and a living screen of their own. She was a member of both the local and state garden clubs and took a great deal of pride in what Mr. Dole termed "her posies" with a twinkle in his eye.

In recognition of her civic contributions to the Peterborough community, her dedicated work in both the local and state garden clubs and for being a role model and mentor to four outstanding daughters—Beth, Edna, Trudie and Dotty—Mrs. Laura Dole was honored with the title "New Hampshire Mother of the Year, 1962."

Around 1940, an Italian stonemason and artisan, L. Pioli, constructed a drain way on the right side of the drive using small round cobbles, hand selected, that he placed one by one. Each spring, the drain way was swept with a hard-bristled broom, cleaning out accumulated silt. Pioli took pride in his stone work, which served its purpose, lasting sixty years.

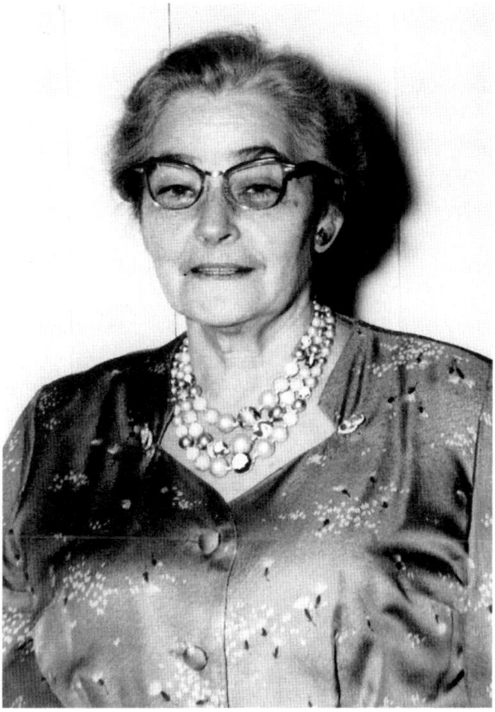

Mrs. Laura H. Dole, Mother of the Year, New Hampshire, 1962. *Courtesy of Dotty Dole Johnson.*

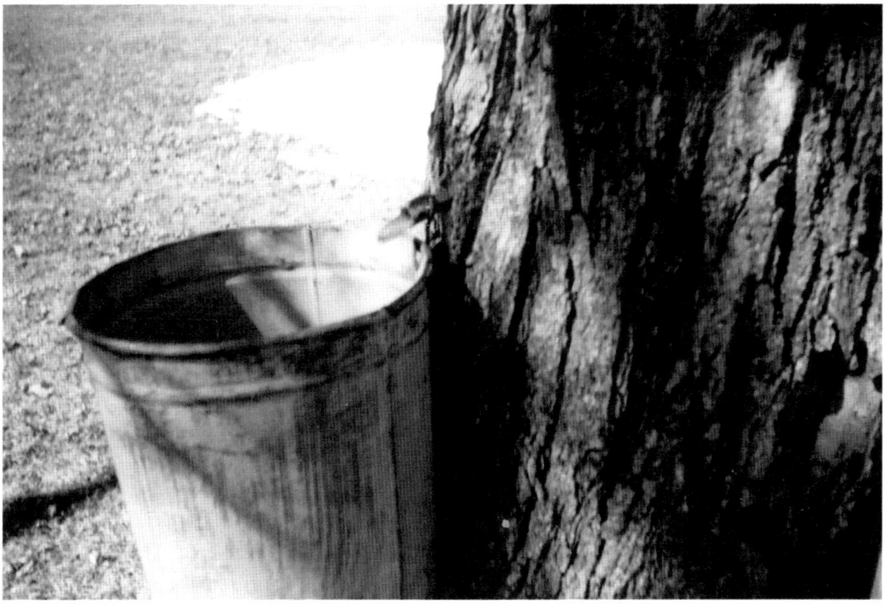

Sugarin' time at the Dole Homestead.

Those gnarled, wide-crowned sugar maple trees that graced the front lawn and lined the driveway had a unique purpose. Along about the first week in March, when rivulets of melted snow ran down the drive and a crow sounded a raucous call from the pasture hemlock, and when the temperature in the daytime hit at least fifty degrees and fell back to below freezing at night, Mr. Dole knew it was time to tap the maples and hang buckets—sugarin' time had arrived.

During a season of good sap runs, Mr. Dole could make six or seven gallons of syrup on a wood-fired cooking range in the old summer kitchen, where stagecoach passengers were fed upon their arrival.

Sugaring isn't easy work, especially when the snow is deep in the first part of the season, but the work seemed lighter when Mr. Dole thought ahead about how good maple syrup would taste on his pancakes. Mrs. Dole was born and raised in Vermont, so no doubt her mother taught her a dozen and one ways to use maple syrup in cooking and baking during the coming year.

Mr. Dole

After moving to Peterborough from Ames, Iowa, in November 1937, I soon became acquainted with our neighbor, Mr. Dole, who owned a small herd of Guernsey cows just three doors above our place on High Street. For my tenth birthday, my dad gave me a Guernsey calf named Vicki, which I stabled in Mr. Dole's barn. That was the beginning of my interest in dairy farming.

Mr. Dole was born on December 9, 1890, in Hartford, Vermont, where his parents operated a dairy farm. However, misfortune struck the Dole family. His mother died when he was very young and then his dad became ill, forcing him to sell the family farm. From that time on, Mr. Dole had to fend for himself. He attended school and worked as a hired man for neighbors and relatives in return for board and room. Setting out on his own, he purchased a small farm near Proctorsville, Vermont.

He met, courted and married Miss Laura Harrington, who taught school. This, no doubt, was the best decision of his entire life. They spent the next fifty-six years together, raising four daughters—Beth, Edna, Trudie and Dotty. The Dole girls would become excellent students, pursuing careers in education, medicine and science.

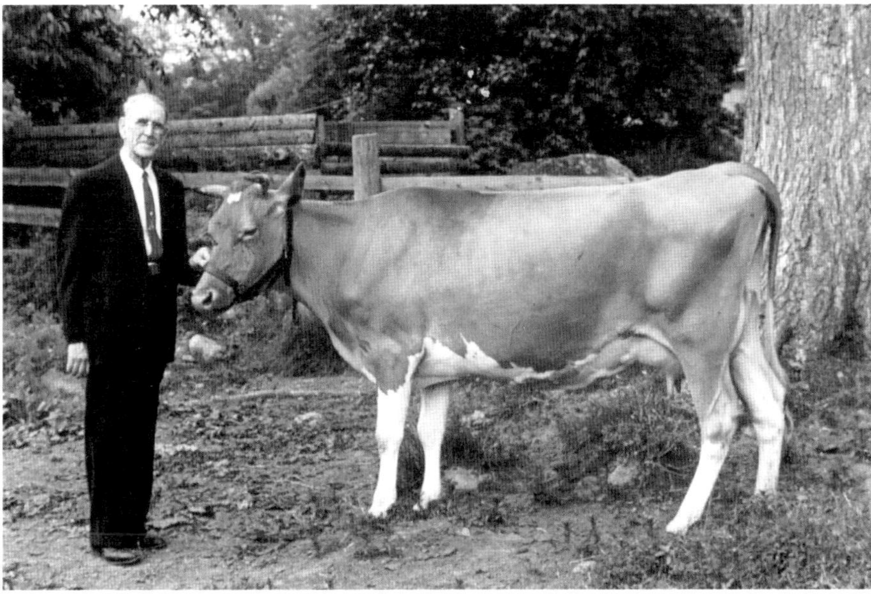

Mr. Fletcher Dole and one of his prize registered Guernsey cows. *Courtesy of Dotty Dole Johnson.*

In 1922, the Dole family moved to Peterborough. He worked as a herdsman on a couple farms, but being of an independent nature, he decided to farm on his own, so he rented a small farm on High Street in Peterborough, stocking it with three grade Guernseys. In 1943, he remodeled the barn and expanded his herd with the purchase of four registered Guernseys. Within a few years, all seven of his Guernseys were purebred.

Mr. Dole delivered Guernsey milk with a deep cream line in glass bottles on a retail route, house to house. However, some of his faithful and long-standing customers came to the house to buy milk in tin gallon pails.

Mr. Dole was hardworking, frugal, honest to the letter, conservative and had countless friends. He knew just about all there was to know about the care of cattle, horses, cats and dogs; how to raise kids and produce fancy maple syrup; and was more than willing to share this information with others. I know because I was there. Frugality crept into his speech, when a simple "yep" or "nope" would do rather than a long song and dance. Should Norman Rockwell have been seeking a model Vermont Yankee, he needn't have looked further.

If one of us kids did something he didn't approve of, as kids will on occasion, he would not gruffly command, "Don't do that!" but would calmly express his request, "I'd just as soon you didn't do that." I can't recall ever hearing Mr. Dole raise his voice, curse or swear.

Being in the company of Mr. Dole, one learned early on a work ethic—that work was not to be avoided or shunned. First and foremost, it is necessary for survival, but of equal importance, work can be enjoyable, was rewarding and bestowed on one a sense of achievement, a reason for being and a way of life.

Two "Mr. Dole-isms" come to mind: "I've never known anybody who worked themselves to death, although I've known a few who died from too much hooch," and "Those who resist, avoid work, or are just plain lazy are doomed to a very unhappy and difficult life."

I still recall a sense of excitement when Mr. Dole came out on the back porch on a warm sunny day in April after finishing lunch and put on his rubber high-top barn boots. "Oh boy," I thought to myself. "We're going to spend the afternoon cleaning cow manure out from under the barn." This was my idea of fun, and I spent many a Saturday afternoon enjoying myself that way. Grammy Kennedy cautioned me, "Tommy boy, you're going to be an old man long before your time."

We neighborhood kids—Ken, Judy, Jackie, Larry and me, to name a few—could on occasion be full of questions: why does this happen, what's that for, what are we doing next? This is pretty typical of kids. We reasoned that if we didn't ask questions, how were we to learn? Mr. Dole had an answer that covered all bases. Patiently, he would advise us, "Keep your eyes and ears open, your mouth shut and you'll find the answers." Of course, he was right.

Mr. Dole also taught me a lesson in being honest early on. I raised Vicki's first heifer calf, which I named Roxy—the one in the same offspring that Doc Tenney predicted would be a bull. When Roxy calved, I had to make room for her in Mr. Dole's barn by selling Vicki. Sometime during her life, she had injured her stifle joint, and although it wasn't a serious injury that in any way affected her milk-producing ability, she was a little lame at times. I advertised Vicki for sale in the state market bulletin, and a local dairyman responded. Mr. Dole's advice was "When Clarence comes to look 'er over, make sure he knows about that stiff stifle joint. He has the right to know what he's buying." I did just that, and Clarence was satisfied with his purchase, paying me $150.

For as long as I can remember, Mr. Dole was custodian at both Central School and the Congregational church. He rose between 5:00 and 5:30 a.m. and drove down to the school to fire up the coal furnaces during the winter months so we'd have warm classrooms. If it had snowed during the night, there were sidewalks to be shoveled. Then it was back home to feed the cows, milk and clean the stable. In the evening, he tended his milk delivery route after doing afternoon chores. He hired a high school lad to help with janitorial work, and when one graduated, another took his place. Classrooms didn't have electric or digital clocks, so Mr. Dole wound each one daily.

Each classroom had six large flower boxes planted with red geraniums. During the school year, we kids kept them watered; however, when summer vacation arrived, all the flower boxes were loaded onto a wagon, and Charlie drew them home. Mrs. Dole oversaw their care during the summer and replaced those when needed. In the fall, they were returned to the classrooms.

When I was growing up in Peterborough, Mr. Dole, in addition to being highly regarded and respected as a typical Vermont Yankee, was also an icon and a celebrity of sorts.

Thornton Wilder, noted playwright, wrote the 1938 Pulitzer Prize–winning play *Our Town* while a resident at the MacDowell Colony, located on upper High Street. There was little traffic back then, so the colonists would stroll to town in the evenings, right down the middle of the street. At about the same time, Mr. Dole would be delivering rich-tasting Guernsey milk with a deep cream line in glass bottles, making a tinkling sound in the metal carrier. Mr. Wilder, being a playwright, was a keen observer of human nature and was inspired to create Howie Newsome, the milkman in the play.

In an interview with Peter Anderson, *Boston Globe* staff writer, Mr. Dole recalled, "I never met Mr. Wilder. I was only a symbol, you see. He didn't try to picture me in the play, but I didn't care to stop them." Of course, it would have made a much more interesting story if Mr. Dole had stated, "Oh yes, I met Mr. Wilder and we discussed various aspects of the play. Even made some suggestions about Howie Newsome's role." However, that was not Mr. Dole's style; he told things the way they were, not what folks wanted to hear. For those of us fortunate to have known Mr. Dole, he was more than a symbol—he was for real.

Mr. Dole attended the premier of *Our Town* when it opened in Boston and played the part of Howie Newsome in a Peterborough Players production. He was interviewed by a German TV crew producing a documentary on the play and was guest of honor at the American Stage Festival. The senior class of Peterborough High School put on the play. "They did a very good job" was his review.

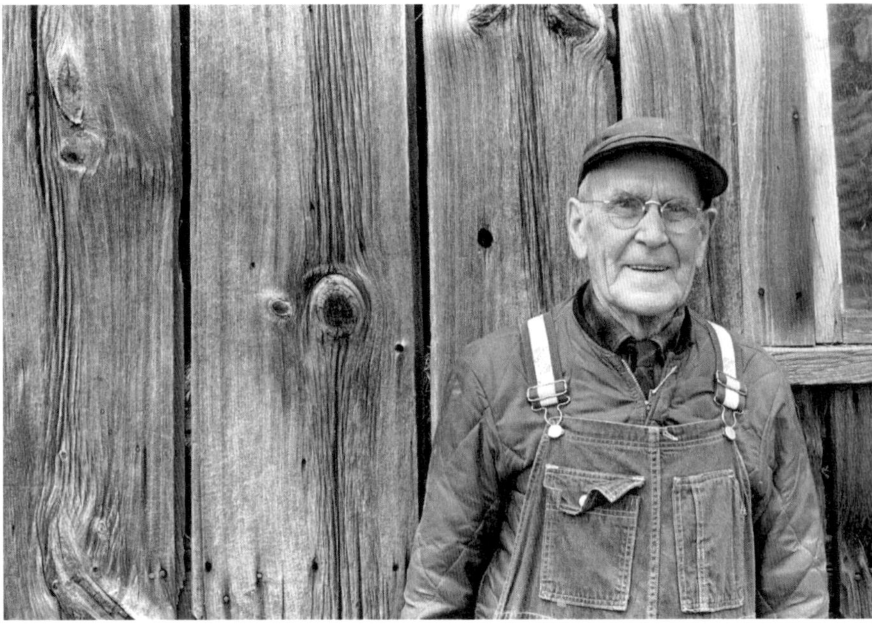

Mr. Fletcher Dole, typical Vermont Yankee. *Courtesy of Molly Backup, Mr. Dole's granddaughter.*

However, Mr. Dole did not take himself or his celebrity status seriously, and when asked about his connection to Howie Newsome, he would just chuckle.

On the morning of October 1, 1973, Mr. Dole milked his Guernseys for the last time, retiring at age eighty-two. Mr. Dole died on May 20, 1980, at age eighty-nine.

The Dole Girls

That the Dole girls were extraordinary scholastically is an understatement. Their spouses were equally talented and gifted. In their respective graduating classes from Peterborough High School, Beth and Trudie were valedictorians; Edna and Dotty were salutatorians.

"Regarding school studies, our parents didn't push us to achieve," recounts Dotty. "It was just expected that we excel." When Dotty, the youngest of the Dole girls, had finished her salutatorian address at the Peterborough High School graduation ceremonies held in the town hall, Mr. and Mrs. Dole overheard someone a couple of rows back mutter, "Well, thank goodness,

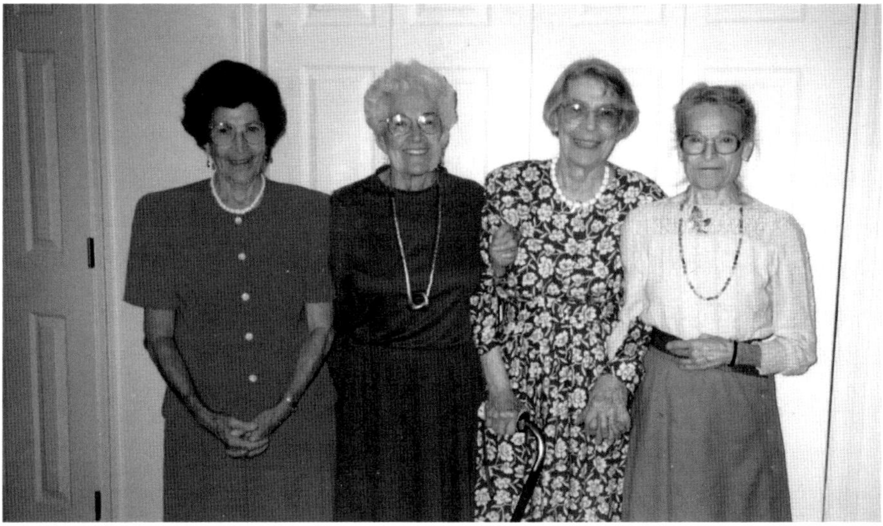

The Dole girls—Dotty, Edna, Beth and Trudie. *Courtesy of Dotty Dole Johnson.*

now that the Dole girls have all been graduated, some other family can share the honors!"

Elizabeth (Beth) graduated from Boston University with a BA degree in Latin. She later earned an MA in education and taught high school Latin. Her husband, Joslin Riford, was a skilled woodcraft artisan, designing white pine furniture.

Edna graduated from Simmons College with a BS degree and received her MD degree from the University of Vermont Medical College, specializing in OB/GYN. Her husband, Phillip Backup, was also an MD and specialized in anesthesiology.

Gertrude (Trudie) graduated from Middlebury College, earned an MA degree in anthropology from the University of North Carolina and a PhD in anthropology from the University of Michigan. Her husband, Robert Carneiro, has a BA, MA and PhD in anthropology. They lived with the Cunicurn Indians in Brazil for five months. "We were their first contact with white people. They were friendly and had the intellect of kindergarten children," Trudie recalls. "It took a while getting accustomed to their daily food fare of various insects and native game animals; also they raised varieties of local vegetables."

Dorothy (Dotty) graduated from Bates College with a BA in biology, and received her MA from Vassar College in biology and her PhD in anatomy from Columbia University. "Miss Hancock, our math teacher and an alumnus of Bates College, encouraged me to enroll and graduate from that institution," Dotty said. She was a professor of anatomy in the College of Physicians and Surgeons of Columbia University. Her husband, Donald Johnson, is an MD who specialized in radiology. "I remember the first CAT scans were grainy and lacked clarity. However, modern technology has opened new horizons in the field of radiology."

School Days

Back in my time, teachers did not have a classroom discipline problem. It was the student who misbehaved, was disruptive, rude or inattentive who had a problem. A teacher would admonish us, "I want your undivided attention!" Our parents paid school taxes, and we were sent to school to learn. Misbehaving, sassing the teacher and being disruptive does not promote learning, either for yourself or your classmates, who numbered between thirty and forty per class. There were no teacher's aides.

It was a given that we respected and paid attention to our teachers, most of whom were women, from grade one through high school, and that misbehaving was not to be tolerated—end of discussion. By no stretch of the imagination were we angels, and on occasion we'd get out of line, in which case we would be disciplined.

The last thing in the world you did would be to go home and complain that your teacher disciplined you, because there was a good chance you'd get disciplined a second time, and complaining to your parents was an open admission of guilt. In those days, the principal or headmaster and parents sided with the teacher, and they were right about 99 percent of the time.

It was given that when we began school as first graders, we would continue, successfully completing twelve grades and graduate from high school. There were forty-two students in the Peterborough High School graduating class of 1950. Smaller surrounding villages closed their schools, busing their students to Peterborough.

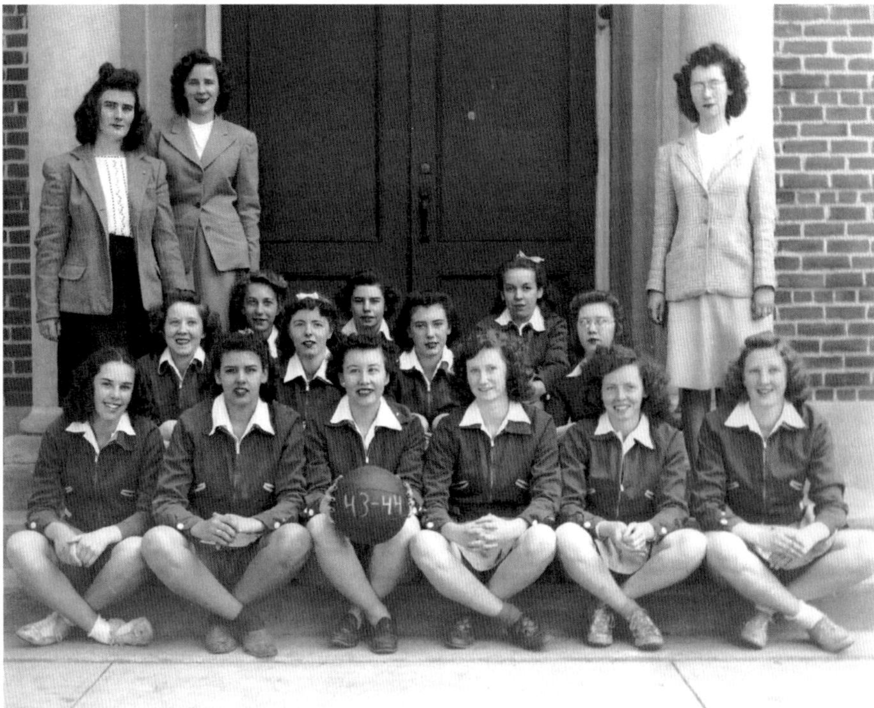

Girls basketball team, 1943–44. *Collection of the Peterborough Historical Society.*

During World War II, when we were in seventh and eighth grades, three seniors dropped out to join the military: Eddie Fontaine, Leo Ledger and Maurice Sumner. After the war, they returned to high school, were excellent students and received their diplomas.

Our math teacher in high school was Miss Florence Hancock; in secret, and when she was miles away from earshot, we called her "Flossie." Miss Hancock was maybe five-foot-two and in top form weighed 110 pounds, at best, but she was a master at discipline. She never raised her voice, but with her sharp tongue, she could cut big guys down to size. In fact, if you were on the receiving end of her wrath, you'd be ever thankful for a wide crack in the floor in which to hide. Because of her reputation, she seldom had to cut us down to size. Miss Hancock was an excellent teacher, respected and well liked by her students.

Our educational teaching aids were standard fare and hadn't changed much since my mom and dad attended one-room schoolhouses. Teachers

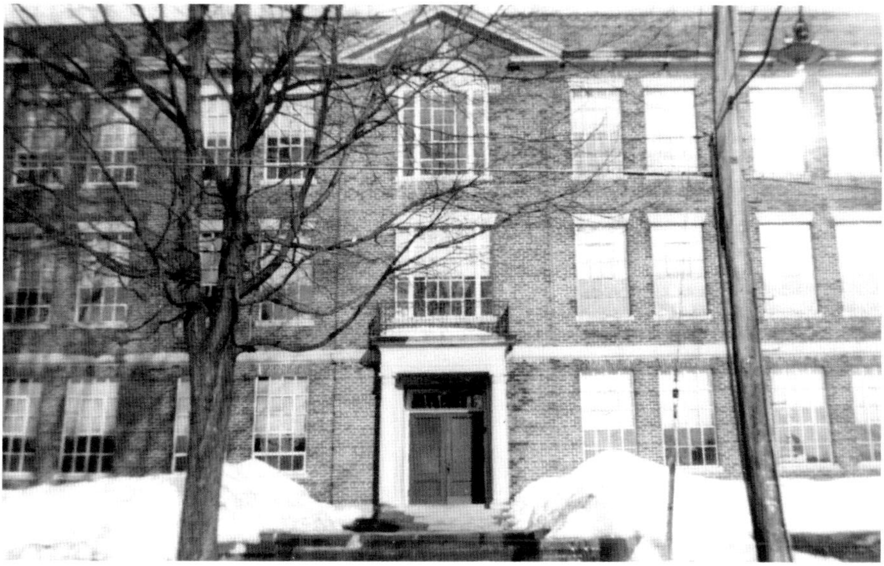

Peterborough High School, built in 1925 and destroyed by fire on December 26, 1971.

wrote on the blackboard, had flip charts and used the mimeograph machine for handouts. Occasionally, an educational film was shown on a 16mm movie projector. Our high school library consisted of one bookshelf eight feet high, running the width of study hall Room 38, along the back wall. Girls interested in becoming secretaries learned how to type on manually operated typewriters; it might have been a good idea if some of us guys had learned how to type, also.

Teachers I Remember

I can remember all my teachers, some better than others. Our first grade teacher was Miss Ricker, a perky redhead. First grade teachers can be very influential because they introduce you to the educational process. Miss Ricker got us off to a great start.

Miss Gertrude Plummer taught second grade, and in those days, much emphasis was put on penmanship; the Palmer Method, it was called. Penmanship paper was lined. Vowels occupied one-half of the space, whereas consonants used the full space, both having an appropriate slant.

We spent considerable time mastering neat penmanship. It's hard to believe that I actually received a certificate stating that I had mastered the mechanics of the Palmer Method of penmanship.

As if it were yesterday, I recall an incident in Miss Plummer's class. My desk was in the middle aisle about four seats from her desk, and we were practicing penmanship. However, taking it to another level, I was writing a story about becoming a dairy farmer.

Miss Plummer, walking up and down the aisles, took note. "Tommy, what are you doing?"

"I'm writing a story, Miss Plummer," I said.

"When you are finished, may I read your story?" She probably was surprised and maybe pleased that a second grader would attempt writing an essay.

Apparently, she was impressed, and she told me so. "Tommy, this is very good writing, and I'm pleased that you take it seriously, so as a reward I want you to read your story to the upper four grades."

This wasn't my idea of a reward because in elementary school there is a definite pecking order, and second graders are at the lower end. I was scared skinny standing in front of each grade reading my story, but I survived.

This was a fortunate happenstance because as we entered high school it was time to think seriously about college and what we wanted to do with the rest of our lives. As for myself, I wasn't bothered with having to make these decisions. I already knew I'd attend the University of New Hampshire, study dairying and someday become a dairy farmer.

Miss Marion Bergeron taught fifth grade. She was a good skier, as were some of her students, so after school on occasion, we'd all go up to the ski slope at the Peterborough Golf Club.

We had some free reading time in fifth grade, and my favorite books were those written by Thornton W. Burgess—*Reddy the Fox*, *Blacky the Crow*, *Jimmy the Skunk* and *Granny Fox*, to name a few. They were talking animals involved in various day-to-day predicaments, quite often with an element of danger involved. One day, Miss Bergeron inquired of me, "Don't you think it's time that you read something a bit more advanced?"

During Easter vacation, Miss Bergeron and her fiancé, Paul Clark, were married, just before he shipped overseas with an armored division. Fortunately, he returned from the war safe and sound. After graduating from college under the GI Bill, he taught secondary education and eventually was appointed school superintendent.

Miss Barbara Hood, our sixth grade teacher, guided us successfully through the last year of elementary school. She put much emphasis on excelling because we were about to advance to junior high school. From time to time she would list the names on the blackboard of those who, in her opinion, were prepared for promotion. We were her first class that she taught, and after retirement, she confided that the future class of PHS 1950 was also her favorite. Kids can be cruel and insensitive, not by design but through thoughtlessness. And that was the case in sixth grade when the craze was moron jokes and one-liners. In the twenty-first century, that would be totally unacceptable, but nonetheless, we had our faults and foibles. That was a chapter in our lives. To reword a quote by Winston Churchill, "this was not our finest hour." Fortunately, this craze did not last long.

With the approach of winter, students at the Central School went into the school nurse's office, where Mrs. Olga Myhaver, RN, gave us each a teaspoon of cod liver oil. I think it had something to do with preventing a winter illness. As I recall, we also received some orange juice to dilute the taste. Cod liver oil ranks dead last on a list of gourmet treats. The spoons were put in hot, soapy water, washed and dried for the next grade; plastic disposable spoons were unheard-of.

We should have been thankful, however, that we weren't students one hundred years ago. Back then, they wore asafetida bags around their necks from the winter's first snowfall until spring arrived. It contained camphor, flowers of sulfur, dried mustard leaves and seeds and a gum resin derived from the root of the *Ferula asafetida* plant. This combination of odoriferous compounds gave off an aroma that was supposed to ward off respiratory germs; it also kept students at a distance from one another! Maybe that was the purpose and mode of action.

Our science, chemistry and physics teacher was Mr. Richard Trufant. He was an excellent teacher, as we learned all we needed to know about these subjects in order to graduate from high school and to go on to college. He had also been a B-29 Superfortress bomber pilot during World War II, so we learned the basics of flying a bomber. I guess this could be considered part of physics under the heading of aerodynamics.

In chemistry class, we did a section on the process of distillation, where a liquid is heated and the more volatile portion is cooled and condensed to yield a refined product. A group of us guys and gals had a Halloween party at my dad and Uncle Frank's camp; the sole beverage was cider. About a half gallon was left over, so after several weeks it turned hard. One of my classmates, Eleanor, and I decided to put our chemistry to practical use. One afternoon, after school let out, Mr. Trufant had gone home and Bill Thibault, the janitor, had finished cleaning the chemistry lab, we set up our distillation unit and distilled the hard cider. We had heard about applejack, knowing it had something to do with hard cider and alcohol.

We made sure the curtain on the chemistry lab window was closed. Then we heated up the hard cider with a Bunsen burner and ran the glass tubing under cold water. Sure enough, the more volatile portion of the hard cider condensed, yielding a distillate with a high alcohol content that dripped into a smaller beaker. Fortunately—and maybe I should state that we were very fortunate—somewhere in our apparatus we used some rubber tubing, causing our end product to have a very vile taste, so vile that it was undrinkable. We didn't know at the time, but our end product tested near two-hundred-proof alcohol, which, if ingested, will do extremely bad things to the optic nerves, like causing blindness. Using good judgment, we dismantled and cleaned our distillery, washing everything down the drain. Nobody was any the wiser, except us because we never tried the experiment again.

Mr. Trufant also taught biology, so during the spring session of school, we did a project on embryology, which studies the growth and development of an embryo. At the time, I was working for Nedlar Farms, a New Hampshire Red poultry farm that specialized in hatching baby chicks. Its hatchery was a battery of incubators that were temperature and humidity controlled, acting much like surrogate mother hens, hatching baby chicks every twenty-one days. Each morning, on the way to school, I stopped at the hatchery, where Ed Wheeler, the hatchery manager, gave me an egg from the incubator for use to examine and study during biology lab. Very little development is observed the first four or five days, but as the days increased, we could observe a developing chick. Mr. Trufant humanely euthanized the embryo after each lab.

As the days advanced, we observed more and more development of the baby chick, which fed on the egg yolk while in its eggshell womb. This proved to be a very educational lab project. Finally, day twenty-one arrived, at which time a live baby chick, dressed in yellow down, picked a bigger and bigger hole in the eggshell and stepped out into the world, which she regarded with black beady eyes. At noon, I took her home, where she joined twenty-four other baby chicks that I was raising under a brooder. Within a day or two, baby chicks were eating a grain chick starter and drinking from a waterer. In six months, she and her flock companions began laying eggs. Actually, "she" turned out to be a "he," named Brigham, and he ruled the roost.

There was no formal class dealing with sex education in high school. At the appropriate age, our parents had the "birds and the bees" talk with us. In Mr. Trufant's biology class, we learned what occurs when an ova and a sperm unite, but that was about the extent of our sex education.

We had the same set of hormones as kids growing up in the twenty-first century. We were no more or less virtuous than teenagers today. However, back in the 1940s, social mores, customs and outside influences were much different than they are today. We didn't have the myriad outside influences relating to sexuality that are present today.

For example, we didn't have TV, MTV, the Internet or advertising with sexual overtones. Lyrics to songs were not explicit; pictures in magazines and ads did not have sexual overtones. Movies did not depict sexuality. What's permissible today was taboo back then. Girls didn't have role models in the entertainment world. Movie actresses back then were in their thirties and forties, fully clothed, and they weren't hopping in and out of bed on the movie screen. Did we consider ourselves puritanical? Not in the least! We were happy, fun-loving, well-adjusted kids who lived each day to the fullest in the 1940s in the Monadnock region. What more can I say?

Boys will be Boys

Yes, like school kids in the twenty-first century, we used to hang out together. One day, we were in Campbell's Drugstore, which had a soda fountain, complete with a marble-topped counter. I don't believe the inside décor had changed much in one hundred years, but why should it, having served its purpose to the community just the way it was all those years. Several of us guys had frappes at the soda fountain; a frappe is the New England version of a milkshake. At twenty-five cents a pop, frappes were considered treats, especially when fifty cents an hour was a good wage in those days.

We were standing outside, shooting the breeze, when someone got a bright idea—I'm not taking credit for this one!

Across the street stood the town hall, the center of official business, dances and basketball games. It was flanked by two majestic elm trees (that was before the Dutch elm disease destroyed so many beautiful trees in town).

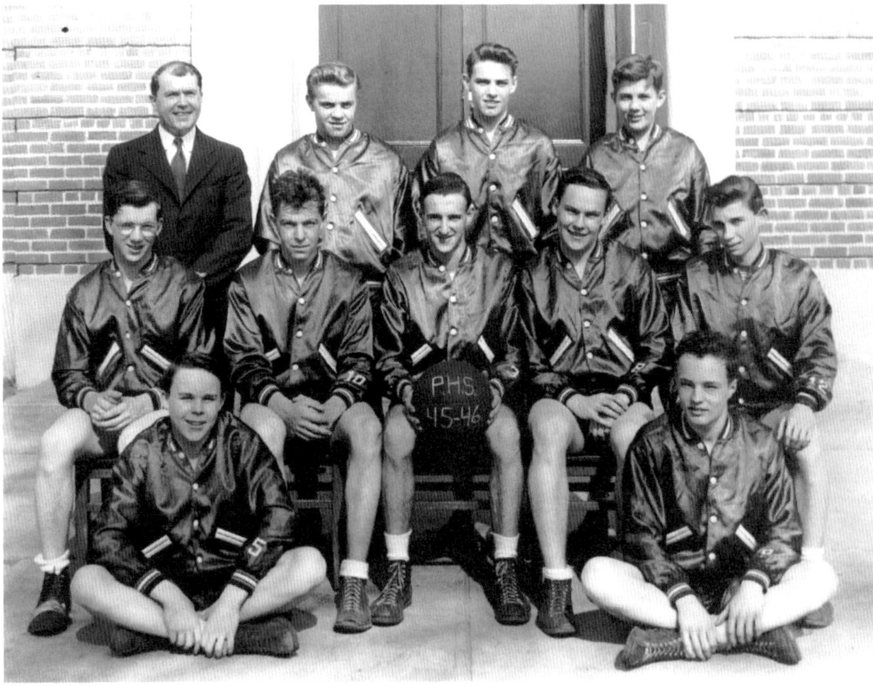

Boys basketball team, 1945–46. *Collection of the Peterborough Historical Society.*

We all started looking up into those tall trees, gesturing with excitement. There was traffic going by, of course, and in a short time, people stopped their cars and were rubbernecking, trying to figure out what was the big attraction. Was it an endangered bird species or even a wild animal from the woods that had taken refuge in downtown Peterborough? About the time that we had traffic blocked back as far as School Street along Grove Street, Chief of Police Albert J. Picard arrived on the scene. In a firm manner, he suggested that all would be better served if we found more constructive ways in which to spend our time. What was up there in those trees? Nothing but tens of thousands of green leaves attached to hundreds of brown branches.

There was a caper I pulled off that at the time I thought was clever, but in retrospect, it was not something I'd tell my grandchildren about. It bordered on irreverence. For whatever reason, I decided I needed the morning off from school. Maybe it was a test I wasn't prepared for. That same morning, the funeral for Eben W. Jones, who had served as selectman and water commissioner in Peterborough, was being held. I asked the high

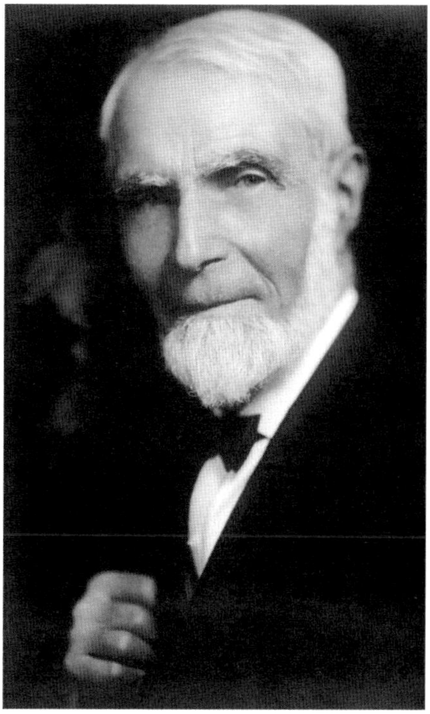

Eben Jones, town selectman, water commissioner, postmaster, president of Peterborough Savings Bank and special court police justice. *Collection of the Peterborough Historical Society.*

school principal, Mr. Gerald Faunce, for permission to attend his funeral, even though I hardly knew the man. "He was a respected town father," I argued, "so I think we ought to pay our respects." I say "we" because there were a couple of my buddies in on this scheme; I wasn't the only guilty party.

What could Mr. Faunce say? If he said, "No, you can't leave school," he'd come off looking like the bad guy, so we got half the morning off from school. Yes, we did actually attend Mr. Jones's funeral!

Elementary School

Our elementary school was called Central School, a three-story building on Vine Street dating back to the mid-1800s. Sixth grade boys, seniors at the Central School, served on the Safety Patrol. I don't recall how we were chosen for this duty. We elected our captain and his assistant, with the rank of lieutenant. We wore Safety Patrol belts, which went about the waist

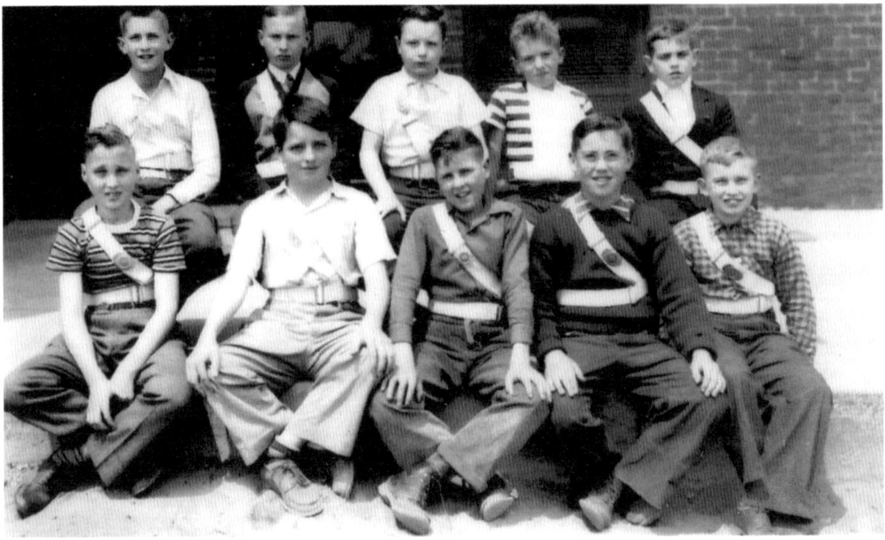

Safety Patrol Squad, Central School, 1943. *From left to right, first row*: Donny Myhaver, Donald Colburn, Donald Paquet, Paul Donovan and Bruce Weston. *Second row*: Bob Clark, Tom Shultz, Henry Smith, Warren Lyon and Joe Burgoyne. *Collection of the Peterborough Historical Society.*

with a crosspiece across the chest and back, adorned with a badge—blue for the captain, red for the lieutenant and silver for patrol members. This gave us authority, which we used with discretion because our duties were to guide students when they were crossing streets; in retrospect, it was a good program.

Classrooms at the Central School were high ceilinged and had six windows, all adorned with flower boxes where geraniums grew. One of the classroom duties, probably the choicest, was to keep them watered. Summer vacation began about June 4 or 5, at which time all the flower boxes were taken out, put on Charlie's wagon and brought to Mr. Dole's house, where they were placed on sawhorses. Mrs. Dole was an ardent gardener; any plant she touched grew. During the summer, she kept the geraniums watered, replacing those plants that had seen better days. Right about Labor Day weekend, the flower boxes were returned to the classrooms, ready for another school year.

The Central School was built on Vine Street in 1887, and when I was in school, it housed the six elementary grades. At the time, it probably was state-of-the-art, with its three stories, constructed entirely of wood, high ceilings and open stairwells. Grades one through three were on the first floor; four through six were on the second. Prior to the dedication of the high school building on High Street in 1925, high school classes were housed on the third story of the Central School. Floors in the classrooms, both halls and stairways, were refurbished each year with some type of oil base wood finish. Girls and boys used separate doors and had separate playgrounds during recess. A fire escape was located on the side of the building that housed grades two and six. During a fire drill, the first three grades exited the building through the entrance doors, while the grades four through six went down the fire escape. It was scary. The fire chief was on hand to time how long it took to evacuate the building.

The Central School was demolished in 1960 to make way for the St. Peter's Church parking lot, and Peterborough High School was destroyed by fire on December 26, 1971.

From the class of 1950, twenty-two continued on to college, two married, six continued in vocational training and twelve joined the military.

Social Life

It's fair to state that back then, teenage boys were not very sophisticated when it came to affairs of the heart. Very few couples went steady or exchanged class rings as a symbol of betrothal. Sometimes they were referred to as a "gruesome twosome," so that left approximately 98 percent of us guys who played the field, dating this girl and that one, but not on a regular basis.

Girls didn't generally kiss on the first date, and if they did, it was considered getting to first base. Holding hands took place if you were that special guy. Of course, there was a certain amount of necking or light petting that took place after a date or dance, but only after you'd been out with a girl a few times. When a girl said "No," she meant "No," not "Maybe"; hookups were unheard-of. That's just the way life was back then in the 1940s.

Saturday night—but not every Saturday night—was when we stepped out, usually to the movies at the GEM Theater and then up to the Goode Shoppe, owned by Thayer Townshend, for a snack and maybe a game or two of pinball. A couple of dollars went a long way when movie tickets were twenty-five cents each and a hot fudge sundae with whipped cream and a sprinkle of chopped walnuts also ran twenty-five cents each. Don't forget to put a couple gallons of gas in the tank of Mom's car at thirty to thirty-eight cents. That was back when fifty to seventy-five cents an hour was a top wage. The seventy-five-cent-an-hour job was a premium.

And then there were the traditional school dances. Looking back, they were actually for the benefit of the girls. We guys were a required accessory, dressed in conservative single-breasted suits (no tuxedos back then). We paid for the dance tickets and corsages, provided transportation and then capped the evening with a snack. It was a plus if the guy was a reasonably good dancer, trying to keep up with gals, who knew the latest pop tunes and dance steps.

Guys at formal dances were akin to the groom at a wedding. Our presence was necessary, but our function was merely ceremonial. The gals had the spotlight and were the center of attention.

Girls were the focal point of the formal dances, dressed in long, flowing and beautiful evening gowns; hopefully, no two would be alike or even similar. Back then, evening gowns were designed with discreet necklines, exposing a minimum of skin, not distracting from the beauty, grace or glamour of the wearer. Evening gowns were not worn to push the envelope to the brink of impropriety.

Traditional high school dances were the Junior and Senior Proms and St. Valentine's Day Sweetheart Ball. If memory serves me correctly, a ten-dollar bill and a couple of ones would cover dance expenses. We didn't rent limos or partake in pre-dance candlelight dinners at fancy—and I might add, expensive—restaurants. A couple of the guys in our crowd had cars, and the rest of us, if fortunate, borrowed our parents' car. Sometimes three couples would crowd into one car; no seat belts were required back then.

One dance I remember in particular was a St. Valentine's Sweetheart Ball. After summoning up courage, I asked Polly if she would like to go with me, and, miracle of miracles, she accepted. Polly was tall, slender and had an aura of regal bearing, in addition to being an attractive gal. She wore a long white chiffon dress that was covered with hundreds of very tiny heart-shaped valentines, matching her red velvet ballerina slippers, and her auburn hair was done in a glamorous upsweep. Polly and Ruthie liked to go on picnics, whereas I think it's fair to say that Bob and I were neutral. However, the girls did pack very tasty picnic baskets with delicious sandwiches—cream cheese and olive tuna fish salad were particularly good. There were potato chips, of course, several varieties of pickles, olives, carrots and celery sticks. For dessert, they had vanilla cupcakes with a generous covering of chocolate frosting. The sandwich bread was trimmed, eliminating those tough crusts. Our beverage of choice was orange, grape, ginger ale or root beer soda pop. On a warm sunny Saturday afternoon in the summer, the four of us, with picnic basket in hand, would hop on our bikes and ride eight miles to Greenfield Lake and the picnic grounds.

Back then in the 1950s, square dancing was very popular in the Monadnock region, when Peterborough hosted three dances a week during the summer, packing the Peterborough Golf Club on Saturdays and Wednesdays and the Bell Studio at North Peterborough on Saturdays. Sometimes you took a date; other times you went stag. It was socially acceptable for the gals to attend square dances without a date.

At Christmastime, Nedlar Farms hosted a dinner party for employees and their wives or girlfriends, so I asked Sally Ann to be my date. We also went to square dances during the summer. It so happened that my co-worker and buddy, Dick, liked a particular girl named Theo, who just happened to be Sally's friend. However, he was too bashful to ask her for a date—that dreaded fear of rejection. I suggested that Sally arrange a date between the two of them. No problem—everything was all set.

I borrowed my parents' car, picked up Dick and headed for Francestown for our dates. About halfway there, he began to get cold feet and was having second thoughts. "Turn around and take me home," he pleaded. "I just know this isn't going to work. She won't like me, we won't have anything to talk about and the party is going to be a total disaster."

"No way," I countered. "If you back out now, we're all going to look bad, and that's not good!"

We were high school cross-country teammates, so I appealed to his competitive spirit. "Think of this as the race that determines the league championship and hang in there," I argued. Reluctantly, he allowed as how he had to make the best of the situation.

As this episode unfolded, Dick and Theo got along just great and had interesting conversations. They began dating and were married right after high school graduation, raising seven children. Now they are grandparents many times over and celebrated their golden wedding anniversary. Dick is forever thankful that I didn't turn around and take him home that night.

Economics influenced how often we dated because there were many demands being made on our paychecks from part-time jobs. We were saving toward college expenses (there weren't student loans back then), and a secondhand car was another big-ticket item. Then there was the purchase of a coveted new or used upland game shotgun or deer rifle, not to mention buying ammo and other hunting items. For those of us who skied, we learned that this could be an expensive sport as well. Skis, bindings, boots, parkas, poles and ski tow tickets were all major expense items, so it was a delicate economic balancing act to maintain one's social status and at the same time support a lifestyle to which we'd become accustomed. It wouldn't be fair to say that we were cheap; frugal is a better term. Maybe we were following the example set by those who originally settled Peterborough, who had survived and prospered because they were frugal and conservative.

I think it's fair to say that for teenage guys back then, the specter of being rejected by a girl loomed like a dark, ominous cloud hovering in the back of our minds.

There were no late school buses back then, so one winter evening, I offered to walk Polly home after a school activity. She lived at the very end of Concord Street, and it was dark and bitter cold, but it was worth the long walk because, to my way of thinking, walking her home was a sign of being accepted. Not surprisingly, the trip back home was not nearly as long or cold.

Entertainment

Before TV became popular, the movies were the main form of entertainment, and I'm told, this was particularly true during the Great Depression years. Money was tight then, but for a dime you could see Clark Gable and Claudette Colbert in *It Happened One Night*, Katherine Hepburn in *Morning Glory* or Spencer Tracy in *Captains Courageous*. Seeing a movie took your mind away from the problems and adversities during those trying times, at least for a couple of hours.

Time has dimmed my memory, but I can recall seeing James Cagney starring in *Yankee Doodle Dandy*, a movie based on the life of George M. Cohan, actor, songwriter, playwright and producer. Cohan wrote hundreds of songs, including the World War I favorite "Over There" and, years earlier, the patriotic song "It's a Grand Old Flag."

When you think about James Cagney, tough-guy gangster types in the movies come to mind. However, he won an Academy Award in 1942 for best actor in *Yankee Doodle Dandy*. I have no idea how he learned the dance routines in this movie because he was not by nature a song and dance man. One of his famous tough-guy lines was "You kilt my brudder, ya dirty rat!"

Speaking of lines in a movie, what is acceptable in the twenty-first century would not pass muster in the 1940s. In the Academy Award–winning movie *Gone With the Wind*, Rhett Butler is standing at the bottom of the staircase of the plantation Tara. Scarlett O'Hara is walking slowly up the stairs when Rhett proclaims, "Frankly, my dear, I don't give a damn!" That line was considered racy, pushing the envelope near the edge.

Peterborough had the GEM movie theater with two shows each night and a Saturday afternoon matinee. As I recall, the interior of the theater was elegant, with carpeted floors, plush chairs and fancy wall hangings. An usher, dressed in either a suit or coat and tie, would escort you to your seat. Today, the GEM is an upscale restaurant.

Back then, when the stage curtain parted and the MGM lion roared, we saw a cartoon, a newsreel and sometimes a short feature, followed by the main billing. There were absolutely no ads.

One bright and sunny but cold January afternoon, the GEM movie theater caught fire. The Peterborough Volunteer Fire Department responded and was able to contain the blaze. There was lots of fire, smoke and water damage to the interior, but the structure itself remained standing.

Adjacent to the theater—and I don't recall that more than six feet separated the two structures—stood Mike Boccelli's cobbler shop. Back then, folks had their boots, shoes, leather goods and accessories repaired rather then throwing them away. Mike was a professional, a cobbler by trade who did a thriving business. When you had a pair of leather boots or shoes that were run down at the heels, needed new soles and some stitch work done, you took them to Mike's cobbler shop. In a week or two, your boots or shoes were as good as new, for about half the price of new ones.

Well, anyhow, Mike's shop was in jeopardy, so a bunch of us guys took over and moved everything out of his shop that wasn't bolted to the floor, taking them across the street to the railroad freight depot, including all the shoes, boots and leather goods that had been repaired or were on the waiting list. We just scooped them up and threw them in boxes because we expected that at any minute the conflagration would break through and catch the shop on fire. Fortunately, this didn't happen, and Mike's shop was spared. However, it took him a while to get all the shoes and boots paired and sorted!

An interesting and unique feature of the inside of his shop was the covering of ivy plants that draped the walls and hung from the ceiling.

For the remainder of the winter, movies were shown at the town hall until the GEM Theater was restored.

Swing Yer Partner

"Okay, boys, let 'er flicker!" That was Ralph Page's call to his band as they played a few chords of a familiar square dance tune. The dance floor was filled within minutes for the contra dance, "Hull's Victory."

Ralph had developed a unique style, being known as the singing square dance caller, his singsong cadence enhancing the rhythm. He was a portly, down-to-earth gentleman, sporting a bushy black mustache. Peering through horn-rimmed glasses with mischievous but good-natured eyes, very little escaped his attention. He viewed square dancing as an art form to be done with grace and decorum, not that he objected to us having a little fun, however.

During the winter of 1945, Ralph held a series of square dance lessons in the Peterborough High School gym, free of charge. This was an era long before rock 'n' roll, disco, rap or line dancing. These lessons created an interest in square dancing, and it was an opportunity to learn from the master; the dances were fast, snappy and intricate, each having an accompanying tune, with no two alike.

Square dancing had its origin in the early 1700s, as immigrants from Europe came to America seeking a better way of life. English immigrants contributed much to square dancing. In Charles Dickens's novel *A Christmas Carol*, we see celebrants performing a contra dance very similar to the present-day Virginia reel at Mr. Fezziwig's Christmas Eve party. The call "Promenade your partner!" and the term "quadrille" are definitely French in origin. "Allemande"—as in "Allemande left your corner lady!"—has its roots in a stately German dance popular in the sixteenth century.

By their very nature, square dances are democratic, because in the course of an evening you have danced with about half the gals, even though you start each set with a partner. More often than not, you don't know your partner, because when Ralph Page's band played the first chords of the upcoming dance, you grabbed a partner and the dance hall filled like magic with four couples forming squares or lining up for a contra dance. Gals from the Monadnock region towns of Greenfield, Francestown and Dublin were always welcome, and going stag was certainly appropriate and socially acceptable. There were no wallflowers, as gals never lacked for partners. Dublin gals, whose parents were from Boston and its suburbs, were "summer folk," owning summer homes around or in the vicinity of Dublin Lake.

Ralph's dance band was one of the best and in a class by itself; three fiddlers, a piano player and an accordionist carried the melody, while a bass player defined the beat. His format was three squares for a set, followed by a contra dance. However, Ralph had it planned so that at the end of the dance, you'd be back with your partner. Age and social status didn't matter, and everybody was equal.

Proper attire back in the 1950s? Guys wore sport shirts, casual trousers, chinos or khakis and loafers—no blue jeans or sneakers. Peasant blouses, long full skirts and ballerina slippers were appropriate for the gals.

After a while, we knew all the dance calls by heart, so some of us young bucks would get a tad smart-alecky and anticipate the next call. In the dance "Red River Valley," after the call "Grand right and left!" we knew the next call would be "And when you get home you swing your own!" Without waiting for Ralph, we'd swing our partners. Bad move! From his vantage point on the stage, he soon picked up on what was going on. At the very last second, he would change the call to "When you get home, de-se-do your corner lady!" Naturally, we got all mixed up and looked foolish. Ralph never said a word, but that mischievous twinkle in his eyes relayed a message: "I gotcha!" Thereafter, we followed his calls because it was Ralph's dance, he was in charge and that's the way it should be.

Then, sometimes, us guys would get a bit rowdy. In the dance "Turkey in the Straw," there's a call—"Now balance your partner!"—which is supposed to be a rather sedate move. We'd spice it up by stomping our feet—right, left, right, left, right—in rapid succession. Trust me, that created some noise! Ralph would halt the band and admonish us, "Whoa fellas, this here's a square dance, not hog wrestlin'!" No sarcasm intended, just a statement of fact.

After intermission, the traditional dance was the contra "Money Musk." You'd best know what you were doing because this was an intricate dance, and you could get mixed up seven ways from Sunday. However, with some friendly pushing and shoving, newcomers would soon pick it up. Sometimes, during intermission, we'd hold an impromptu lesson for first-time dancers. After that, it was second nature, and once learned, never forgotten.

If only we could turn back the hands of time—not an original statement, but nonetheless true. To have the same group of dancers who had so much fun and enjoyment at the Peterborough Golf Club, with Ralph calling the dances and his band in full swing, would be the best of times back then in the 1940s!

The last dance of the evening was "Darlin' Nelly Gray," and the closing call was "Promenade around the hall and when you get home, swing your darling Nelly Gray!" As the last musical notes drifted out into a balmy summer night, Ralph bid us farewell with: "That's all folks, see you next Saturday night."

Radio

Back in the 1940s, TV was virtually unknown, at least to the average household. In 1875, an American inventor, G.R. Carey, began research that would later evolve into TV, and by 1930, John L. Baird, a Scotch inventor, had transmitted TV images from England to the United States. Bell Telephone Laboratories and General Electric were developing TV, but the pictures were of low quality and had little entertainment value.

In the 1930s and through the '40s, radio was the favorite family entertainment on a daily basis. We'd all gather around the big cabinet-style RCA, Motorola, Philco or Zenith radios to listen to the news followed by our favorite programs.

What I remember most about radio is that it forced you to use your imagination as you followed the audio script. Sound effects were real, and who can forget the sound of the Lone Ranger's horse, Silver, and his faithful Indian partner, Tonto, as they pursued bank robbers and brought cattle rustlers to justice? In your mind's eye, you visualized all the action that was taking place, linking what you heard with what your mind told you was happening. As radio listeners, we became program creators. Sadly, that's not the case when viewing TV, where we sit in front of the TV screen and are spoon-fed fare, some of which is not all that great.

In our household, the comedy radio programs were the favorites, although Grandma Kennedy enjoyed the afternoon soap opera *Just Plain Bill.*

On Sunday night at 7:00 p.m., Jack Benny and his cast were guests in our living room. Don Wilson, with his booming voice, was the ideal announcer; Rochester, the ever-patient valet and chauffeur of an aging Maxwell car; Phil Harris, the band leader who liked the sauce and his favorite song, "That's What I Like About the South"; and Dennis Day, the gullible Irish tenor. Then there was Mary Livingston. On the program, she wasn't Jack's wife or even his girlfriend, but she kept the program on an even keel, bringing

Jack down to earth, giving him his comeuppance and pricking his balloon of vanity. She was the counterbalance to Jack's foibles—his being cheap, vain and a lousy violin player. In real life, she was actually Mrs. Jack Benny.

Jack got his biggest and longest laughs when he was the fall guy, the butt of his own jokes, putting himself down or coming out the loser of a historical argument with Don Wilson. None of the other cast members were ever put down; it was only Jack, which explains why he was so likeable and funny. We all knew that in real life Jack was a very generous man, modest to a fault, as well as a gifted musician. The humor is derived from the contrast and his being the master of timing. In the script, Jack would never, ever say anything mean-spirited, cruel or risqué about another person just for the sake of a laugh. He held this high standard over the span of forty years as a comedian and was respected by his peers. Insofar as being vain, he supposedly wore a toupee and never aged past his thirty-ninth birthday.

His funniest joke, the one that got him the longest and most laughs? In the book *The Jack Benny Show*, author Milt Josefsberg writes that Jack's choice would have to be the following:

> *Hold-up man: Your money or your life!*
> *Jack: Hmmmmm. (Long, very long, pause.)*
> *Hold-up man: Quit stalling, I said, "Your money or your life!"*
> *Jack: I'm thinking it over!* [This gag was aired March 28, 1948.]

Who can forget Fibber McGee and Molly on Wednesday night and how we knew that sooner or later Fibber would open that closet door and all its contents would come crashing and rattling out. It always happened, and by today's standards, it was old and corny, but it gave us enjoyment, and what's so wrong with that?

Fred Allen and Jack Benny were always bickering and feuding, putting each other down on their respective programs, trying to outdo the other guy with criticism. The humor here lies in the fact that in private life, they were the best of friends, each respecting the other, but on the radio they sounded like the Hatfields and McCoys.

There were other programs that come to mind, such as the *Great Guildersleeve*, Henry Aldrich, George Burns and Gracie Allen. The creaking door as the Shadow proclaims, "Only the Shadow knows the evil that lurks in the hearts of men!"

On radio, the commercials were short, to the point, infrequent, non-irritating and effective.

Radio brought baseball into our homes when games were played during the daytime, although we did see night games at Fenway Park and Braves Field in the late 1940s. Naturally, you were either a Braves or Red Sox fan, and you knew all the players, their position and their stats. Players, for the most part, began and ended their baseball careers with the same team because they didn't jump from one team to another. The same applied to the managers; Billy Southworth managed the Boston Braves and Joe Cronin the Red Sox for as long as we could remember. It was something we could count on from one year to the next.

Back then, Major League Baseball consisted of the American League and the National League, with eight teams in each. The National League included the Boston Braves, New York Giants, Brooklyn Dodgers, Philadelphia Phillies, Cincinnati Reds, Chicago Cubs, St. Louis Cardinals and Pittsburgh Pirates. The American League had the Boston Red Sox, New York Yankees, Philadelphia A's, Washington Senators, Cleveland Indians, Detroit Tigers, Chicago White Sox and St. Louis Browns.

At the end of the season, the winner of the American League played the winner of the National League in the World Series, taking four games out of seven to decide the champion. There weren't any league playoffs or wild cards, and the series was usually decided during the first week in October. Of course, all the games were outdoors on natural grass.

There was a minor-league team, the Nashua, New Hampshire Dodgers, a farm club in the Brooklyn Dodger system, that we enjoyed watching because they had a very talented rookie, Jackie Robinson. When Jackie got on base, we knew he would try to steal second base; it wasn't a matter of if, but when. He'd take a long lead, arms outstretched, dancing back and forth to rile the pitcher. Prior to serving as an army officer, he had been a track star at UCLA in the one-hundred-yard dash, so he was quick. With the fast start and speed, he usually stole second base, going in headfirst. He wasn't quite as successful stealing against lefty pitchers, but they weren't safe because he was that fast. The following year, he played for the Montreal Dodgers in the International League, and in 1947, he was signed by Branch Ricky to play for the Brooklyn Dodgers.

During the World Series, we were allowed to listen to the radio broadcast in study hall Room 38, provided we kept the volume down. As with radio programs, we visualized what was happening by listening to the sportscasters who brought the game to life in vivid descriptive terms.

It was the 1946 World Series! Who can forget the spirited voice of Curt Gowdy holding us spellbound with play-by-play baseball live from Fenway Park? What a disappointment! Our beloved Boston Red Sox lost to the St. Louis Cardinals, four games to three. Howie Pollet, pitching for the Cardinals, won twenty-one games that year. Two years later, we were again frustrated. The Boston Braves lost the World Series to the Cleveland Indians, four games to two.

While World War II was raging in both the European and Pacific Theaters of operation, we tracked the horrific events, day by day, listening to radio newscasters.

Holidays

Independence Day

In American history class, we learned that on the Fourth of July 1776, our founding fathers signed the Declaration of Independence, the cornerstone of life, liberty and the pursuit of happiness, as we know it today, under our democratic form of government. We also learned at an early age that it was the one day of the year that we could set off firecrackers and fireworks to our hearts' content, without fear of the law.

Back then, it was a fireworks buyers' bazaar, with the only limiting factor of how much you could buy being the jingle in your pocket; there was no law prohibiting their sale.

Basically, a firecracker is a cardboard cylinder packed with gunpowder, with a paper cord fuse attached, that came in three sizes: one, two and six inchers. Don't forget the cherry bombs, which were small cardboard balls packed with gunpowder and a fuse that make a thunderous racket when lighted and tossed down storm drains.

Before we began setting off our firecrackers, Mom and Dad would caution us, "Now you be careful!" I recall only one accident where a kid got injured, but looking back at some of our antics, it's a wonder there weren't more of them. Using matches to light the fuses was time-consuming and tedious, so we used a punk stick, which smoldered constantly. You could also buy a string of half-inch firecrackers that sounded like a machine gun when ignited.

At night, groups of neighbors gathered in backyards for a picnic of hot dogs, hamburgers, salads, potato chips, deviled eggs and lemonade. Gas grills were unheard-of, so a small fireplace grill was used for cooking, and afterward we'd roast marshmallows over red-hot coals.

As the sun set behind Mount Monadnock, one of the adults set up the various aerial fireworks—Roman candles, pinwheels and skyrockets—and we kids would light up our sparklers. Then, when it was dark and the fireflies appeared, an adult would set off the fireworks to shouts of delight and excitement and many, many exclamations of "oohs" and "aahs" as the last of the fireworks burnt themselves out.

Christmas

There is something special about the Christmas season that goes beyond receiving presents. It is all about family being together and sharing the joy and excitement of the Yuletide.

When my sister, Ann, and I were growing up, we were staunch believers in Santa Claus, so it was hard to go to sleep knowing that sometime during the night Santa would arrive, fill our stockings, leave that special present we had

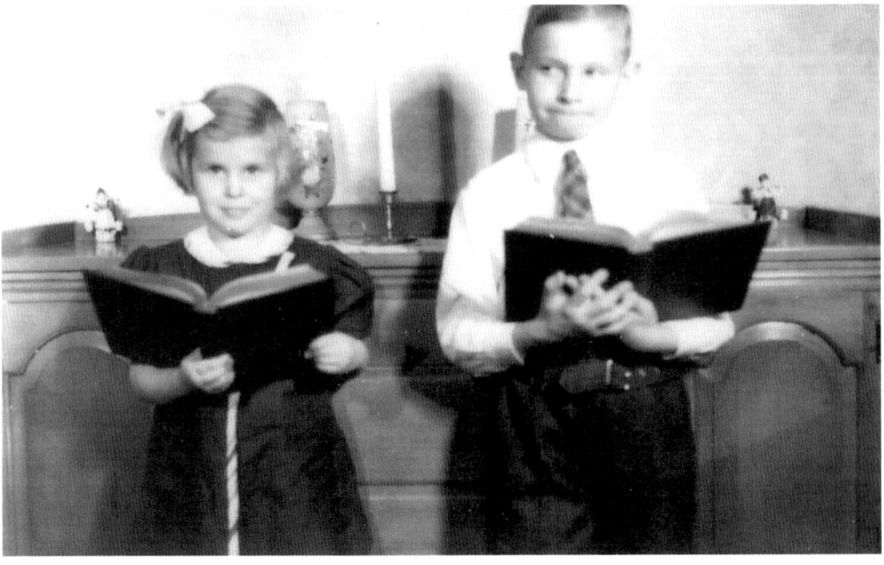

Tom and Ann Shultz, Christmas 1940.

asked for, eat his sandwich and drink the glass of milk left for him. Then he would jump back into his sleigh, yell to his eight reindeer and be on his way. Back then, Rudolph the Red-Nosed Reindeer hadn't yet joined the team. The anticipation and thrill of what the morning would offer was almost too much to bear, but fortunately sleep would overtake us.

One memorable Christmas Eve stands out; it was probably 1940 or 1941. My mom, dad, Ann and I were driving around Peterborough to admire all the houses with Christmas decorations, ornamented trees, lights and Christmas scenes. At the corner of Main and Grove Streets, next to the town hall, stood a gigantic blue spruce tree that the Highway Department crewmembers always decorated with hundreds of colored lights at Christmastime. When this tree was lit, you knew the Yule season had arrived.

Folks really outdid themselves with decorating back then, and there was a light snow falling, which made for a typical New Hampshire Christmas.

One Christmas Eve, we were driving down Concord Street, gazing at and admiring all the Yuletide sights when, lo and behold, there was Santa Claus walking along the sidewalk, shouldering a huge sack filled with toys and presents. Ann and I were at an age when we were firm believers in an actual living Santa, and there he was! We just knew he was on his way to our house, so we told Dad we wanted to go straight home and be in bed before he arrived. We high-tailed it home to High Street, got into our PJs and were heading upstairs when the doorbell rang.

Dad answered the door, and there stood Santa, big as life and twice as natural. This had to be the most exciting and memorable Christmas Eve of our lives! He was all that we imagined him to be, dressed in red trousers, jacket and jaunty cap trimmed with white fur. He had a full white beard, an ample middle and wore shiny black boots. After telling him what we wanted for Christmas, we both scampered up to our beds, where sleep was slow in coming.

A few years later, when we had become sophisticated and worldly, Mom told us that the Christmas Eve Santa was actually Mr. Richard Price, editor of the *Guernsey Breeders' Journal* and one of Dad's colleagues.

Back in the 1940s, most of the Christmas decorations were the traditional tree, festooned with lights, ornaments, tinsel and Christmas candle lights in windows. There was very little outside decorating done, with the exception of a live tree with lights. My mom and sister did the tree decorating, while my task was going forth to find just the right size and shape of tree in the woods.

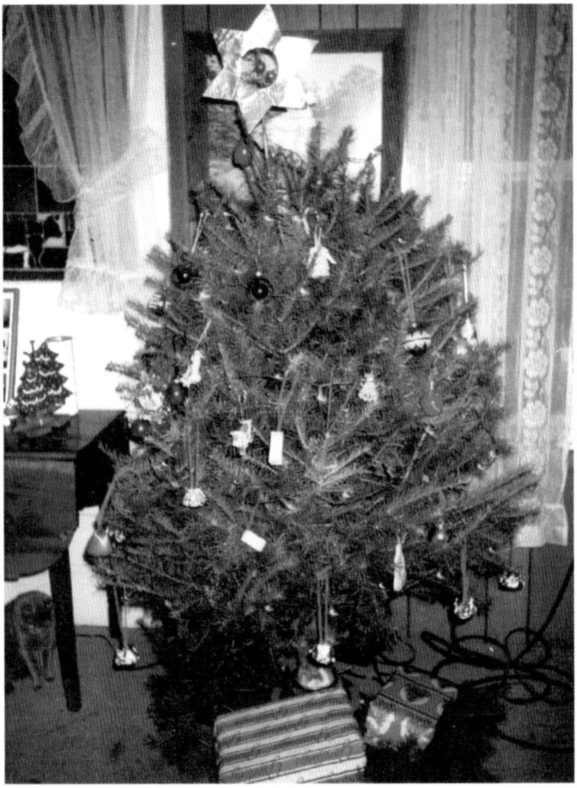

My parents' first tree in 1930.

Henry Lord, who lived on Old Sheet Road, put up a spectacular life-sized manger scene in front of his residence. This was a must-see each Christmas for Peterborough residents, a tradition that many remember years later.

Thanksgiving

For our first Thanksgiving in Peterborough, in 1937, we were invited to Uncle Karl and Aunt Madge Musser's for dinner. Other guests were the Bunces, the Prices and the Charles Cummings, none of whom had relatives living nearby. Thus began a tradition that continued for many years. The women of each family brought the food for a traditional Thanksgiving feast, while Uncle Karl provided an ample and plump fresh turkey. For dessert, the offering was a variety of tasty homemade pies: lemon, chocolate, pumpkin, banana cream, apple and cherry.

As the guest list increased each year, an additional bird—and a large one at that—was needed, so each family took turns contributing a second turkey. When it was my dad's turn, one of his friends who raised White Hollands gave him a live bird. Dad took the crated turkey to a poulterer to be dressed. A recent and early snowstorm had blocked the entrance to his shop. "Just bring the crate through the front door," he instructed my dad. You've guessed by now what happened. Somehow the turkey escaped, flew around the living and dining rooms and kitchen, knocking over lamps, upsetting bric-a-brac and scattering feathers and droppings.

Sometime during the first two weeks of November, all the Guernsey wives met at Aunt Madge's to plan who was going to bring what. Uncle Karl had a standing request, "Make sure Helen [my mom] brings a couple of lemon meringue pies." They were his favorite—tangy and tasty, with a light flaky crust topped with fluffy meringue, lightly browned on top. They did Mom proud.

Each year, additions were made to the guest list as new families moved to Peterborough for employment at the Guernsey Club. It wasn't long before the number of guests outgrew the upstairs dining room, so the dinner was moved to the basement, which had been remodeled into a spacious and comfortable family room. Uncle Karl had an extensive collection of ornate beer steins decorating a ledge that encircled the room.

After all were seated, Uncle Karl offered grace: "Our Heavenly Father, we thank thee for the bounty set before us, and for the gifts you've bestowed upon us during the past year, and for the fellowship we share today with family and friends. Bless those who have prepared this feast. Amen."

Easter

No discussion of holidays would be complete without including Easter. For us kids, there is the anticipation of Christmas, with presents and the midnight arrival of Santa Claus. The Fourth of July brings the excitement of firecrackers, skyrockets and Roman candles. And who can forget the aroma of a roasting turkey on Thanksgiving?

For Christians, Easter is spiritual in nature, having its origin over two thousand years ago, celebrating Christ rising from the dead. To those of the Jewish faith, Passover coincides with Easter during the first month of the Jewish year. The feast of Passover lasts eight days, from the fourteenth to the twenty-first of the month Nizan. This coincides with the first full moon of spring.

Then there is a third dimension of Easter, which is pagan in nature. Venerable Bede, an English historian of the eighth century, reasoned that the word Easter is derived from the Norse term *Eastre*, meaning "the arrival of spring and new life." Hence, we have the Easter bunny, known for fertility, and eggs of varied colors denoting the sun's rays and aurora borealis.

So actually, we kids celebrated Easter in a pagan way, hunting Easter eggs and eating more candy and chocolate bunnies than we should.

However, as we became older and attended Catechism classes taught by the Catholic nuns from Keene each Saturday morning, we learned the true meaning of Easter.

First order of the day on Easter morning was attending Catholic Mass at St. Peter's Church. Hunting Easter eggs and eating candy would have to wait. We celebrated Easter first as Christians, and then we gave the pagan way its due.

World War II

When Pearl Harbor was bombed on December 7, 1941, President Franklin D. Roosevelt proclaimed, "This will be a day that will live in infamy." War was declared on December 8 with only one dissenting vote from both houses of Congress. On December 11, 1941, both Germany and Italy declared war on the United States.

Mr. Dole had a radio in the barn to listen to the world news while doing chores. One evening in the fall of 1941, after I'd finished my chores, I started for home. He said, "You should listen to the following program." It was a public address by the United States ambassador to Japan, Joseph C. Grew. Grew was a Harvard graduate and a career foreign diplomat, having served under four presidents from 1904 to 1941. I don't recall what the ambassador said, but it sounded ominous, and I remember that the text of Ambassador Grew's speech worried Mr. Dole. A point of interest was that Ambassador Grew owned a summer residence in the neighboring village of Hancock, eight miles from Peterborough.

In a radio address to the nation, President Roosevelt proclaimed, "We are going to win the war and we are going to win the peace that follows." Defeating the Axis Powers and preserving our way of life was our ultimate goal, after which we would help rebuild the countries ravaged by war. President Roosevelt did not intend to repeat the same mistakes made by the victorious allies following World War I, when Germany was stomped on and beaten down with the burden of hefty war reparations. At the time, this type of treatment of the defeated Germans seemed like a good idea, but it only spawned the spirit of German nationalism, Adolph Hitler and the Nazi party—and ultimately World War II.

We had been attacked by aggressors, and our way of life, liberty and the pursuit of happiness was in grave jeopardy. The entire nation was caught up in an unprecedented spirit of patriotism. In an address to Congress on January 6, 1941, President Roosevelt proclaimed that the entire world should be founded on four freedoms: freedom of speech, freedom of religion, freedom from want and freedom from fear. The attack on Pearl Harbor gave the "four freedoms" a sense of urgency and a greater meaning.

After December 7, tens of thousands of young men and women enlisted in the armed forces of the United States. Between December 7, 1941, and December 31,1946, 16,353,659 of them would have served their country. For the first time, women left the home and joined the workforce in defense plants, building tanks, ships, aircraft, armaments and munitions, just to mention a few. Clara Taylor was the first woman certified as a welder; she helped construct war ships at the Brooklyn Navy Yard. Everybody in America was making sacrifices for the war effort, beginning with President Franklin Roosevelt and trickling on down to the average citizen. The president and his wife, Eleanor, had four sons who served in the military in combat zones with distinction.

Everyone had either a close family member or members who were in the armed forces or a close friend who was serving.

Banners with stars for each member of a household serving in the armed forces appeared in front windows of houses. As the war dragged on, gold stars began to appear far too often: All gave some. Some gave all. The Selective Service Act of 1940 was amended on December 19, 1941, decreeing that males ages twenty to forty-four could be drafted to serve in the armed forces. Under an amendment to the Selective Service Act, the upper limit was lowered to age thirty-seven. With parental permission, seventeen-year-olds could enlist in the navy or U.S. Marine Corps, so lots of guys dropped out of high school to enlist. Some earned a GED while in the service, and others returned to high school after the war.

Many Civilian Conservation Corps (CCC) recruits enlisted in the armed forces before the war began. The CCC was a quasi-military unit, so they were familiar with regimentation, taking orders and the concept of discipline. They had also learned the value of teamwork, which is a vital element of the military. Many CCC recruits had learned a vocational trade that was a vital part of the armed forces, ranging from auto mechanics to X-ray technicians. It's been said that for every man in combat on the firing line, there are nine others in a supporting role.

Just about everything you could think of was rationed: gas, sugar, coffee, heating oil and kerosene, meat, canned goods and anything rubber, just to name a few. Everybody, including babies, was issued a ration book containing stamps needed to purchase rationed items during a given time period. Rationing was administered by the Office of Price Administration (OPA) and must have been a bookkeeping hassle for all concerned, but as the common saying of the day was, "Don't you know there's a war on?"

Because gas was rationed, the smallest amount allotted per week was for pleasure, with larger amounts allowed for business purposes. Farmers had adequate amounts to fuel tractors because food production was so vital to the war effort. Although folks grumbled about rationing, they knew it was necessary to win the war, and this was by and large the attitude of the war years.

Canned goods were rationed, so many families had victory gardens to raise home-grown vegetables. My dad and I had a large garden. Memorial Day was planting time, after which it was my job to do the weeding and later harvest the produce of beans, tomatoes, carrots, peas, squash, corn and cukes. I recall how my mom and grandma put up hundreds of jars of canned vegetables, fruit, jams and jellies. I can still smell the spicy, pungent aroma of apple butter, dill and bread-and-butter pickles. Remember, this was long before home freezers were commonplace. I had a Guernsey cow, Vicki, and later her daughter, Roxy, that produced milk and cream for our family. I also had a flock of twenty-five New Hampshire Red hens for egg production. They were good layers, so I had extra eggs to sell, with home delivery. Mrs. Lenore Hunter loaned me her henhouse for my flock, and sixty years later, I regret I didn't give her a dozen eggs from time to time in exchange for using the henhouse. After the hens stopped laying eggs, they ended up in the stew pot, and I got another batch of pullets.

Because metal of all kinds was vital to the war effort in the production of vessels, tanks, trucks, guns of all description and other implements of war, vast scrap metal drives were organized to assemble these materials in central locations for future use. Ironically, in the late 1930s, the Japanese had been major buyers of U.S. scrap metal.

Collecting milkweed pods was another activity that we kids participated in to help the war effort. In the early fall, the pods attached to milkweed plants ripened, which produced a light, filmy product that was used in the production of life jackets, due to its buoyancy. We'd take gunnysacks filled with pods down to the Peterborough Basket Company. This is a further demonstration of how the entire American populace was totally behind the war effort.

In school, we had scrap metal and paper drives, competing to see which classes would collect the most tonnage. Out of fairness, the senior class teamed up with the first grade, the junior class with the second grade, etc. Collecting old rubber tires was a major effort because our source of raw rubber in the Far East had been taken over by the Japanese.

Metal of all kinds was a scarce commodity for civilian consumption because the major use was needed for the war effort. Plastic was used more and more to replace metal for consumer products, and while we preferred metal to plastic, we didn't complain because winning the war was more important. We thought that plastic appeared overnight due to the war effort, but actually the concept of plastic material had been around for several decades. John W. Hyatt and his brother, Isaiah S. Hyatt, founded the Albany Dental Plate Company in 1870 to manufacture plastic, one of the first of its kind in the United States.

Petroleum products were major commodities needed to fuel the United States war machine, and a number of methods were used to conserve energy. Both gasoline and fuel oil were rationed. In our household and most others, upstairs bedrooms weren't heated, or the thermostat was turned way down, and parts of the downstairs were not used during the winter. To supplement heat, many woodstoves appeared, and the sale of firewood took a big jump. An extra blanket at bedtime would also save fuel oil.

For us kids looking to make some spending money, we worked countless hours hauling and stacking firewood in basements, garages and utility sheds.

Financing a war costs millions upon millions of dollars, so the U.S. government came up with an ingenious idea to help raise money: War Savings Bonds. For $18.75, you bought a bond, backed by the Treasury Department, which would mature in ten years with a value of $25.00, yielding approximately 3 percent. Coming up with $18.75 was difficult, so the government sold savings stamps for ten or twenty-five cents, which would be pasted in a savings book, and when the book was filled, you received an $18.75 War Bond (they were also known as Savings Bonds). Many of us paid for our college educations in this manner because these bonds could be cashed in earlier with a reduced return; they had to be held at least one year. Filling up the saving books with stamps was a natural gift when you tried to think of something to give to a friend or relative on his or her birthday or as a Christmas present. Perhaps it wasn't an exciting gift, but you had to consider the future benefits and pride in helping the war effort.

Each and every town had a cadre of air raid wardens. The chief air raid warden in Peterborough was Major A. Erland Goyette, assisted by deputy John E. Cass, and during air raid drills, it was their job to make sure no lights were shining from any house. They wore steel helmets as they patrolled the pitch-black streets. Looking back, I don't believe the German Luftwaffe had any military targets lined up in Peterborough, nor did it have bombers with range enough to get here. But we asked no questions, just did what we were told because "there was a war going on." That pretty much was the spirit of the day.

Speaking of bombers and military targets brings to mind the lookout posts. Peterborough had one on East Hill Road near Pack Monadnock Mountain and another off Cheney Avenue in an apple orchard, which became a housing development in the postwar era aptly named Lookout Hill. The purpose of these lookout posts was to spot and report the presence of all aircraft by phone to Grenier Field, an air force base in Manchester, because radar was still in the research stage of development.

If memory serves me right, they were manned twenty-four-seven year round in all kinds of weather by teams of at least two or more persons. Some volunteer was responsible to see that the lookout posts were manned. To help identify aircraft, there were binoculars and an identification chart of both friendly and enemy aircraft, showing a side view of each plane. Plane watchers had to know the difference between a P-47 Thunderbolt and a German Stuka. Plane spotters brought sandwiches, snacks and a thermos of coffee. Dog-eared playing cards were available for games. At the sound of an approaching aircraft, somebody would spot and identify the plane and report its presence to Grenier Field. In the postwar era, this air base was deactivated in a round of base closures.

Few, if any, planes flew over Peterborough without being reported, a further example of how ordinary folks took the war effort seriously. There's no doubt that there was an element of socializing while on duty as plane spotters, but they got the job done. That's all that was necessary.

Occasionally, a convoy of army 6x6 trucks carrying soldiers would come through town. Somewhere along the line, they would come to a stop, and we kids would chat with the men. Quite often, the soldiers would give us money, and we'd ride our bikes back to a store and buy them candy bars, snacks and soda pop. They really appreciated this, and looking back some sixty years, you have to wonder which ones of those nameless faces returned home alive and which ones came back wounded or disabled.

News about how the war was progressing reached us via radio newscasts, newspaper and, finally, through magazines.

I used to listen to Lowell Thomas every evening at 6:45 p.m. before going up to Mr. Dole's to do my evening barn chores. Because there was no TV, the GEM movie theater showed films every night. Prior to the feature attraction, there would be a newsreel showing the progress of the war, followed by a cartoon and sometimes a short feature. Seeing a color film would be a special treat for, as I recall, the price of a dime.

One of my cousins in Cincinnati, Ohio, was watching the newsreel at a Saturday movie matinee. The cameraman showed a squad of marines landing on Iwo Jima on February 19, 1945. He focused close in on one particular marine, who turned his head. My cousin yelled out, "Hey, that's my brother Jerry!" The next day the movie theater manager replayed, in slow motion, the newsreel for my aunt and uncle. Sure enough, there was Jerry, proof that he did get ashore. Many U.S. Marines didn't make it that day. Nearly six thousand died before Iwo Jima was secured on March 26.

I don't remember VE Day, May 8, 1945. All of us were so thankful that the fighting in Europe was over, but we also realized that a momentous, costly and bloody battle to conquer the Japanese mainland remained. Our military leaders had this warning: "We know that the Japanese military, as well as the civilian population, will fight to the last in defending the Land of the Rising Sun." That prediction was ominous, and as my cousin Marine Sergeant Jerry Kennedy predicted when we bade him farewell at the train station, "the next landing is going to be the toughest one yet."

On August 6, 1945, the first atomic bomb was dropped on Hiroshima, Japan, and on August 9, a second one was dropped on Nagasaki. August 14, 1945, was V-J Day, with a formal unconditional surrender of Japan on September 2 on board the USS *Missouri*.

I do remember V-J Day and will for the rest of my life! It was the end of World War II, an end to seeing our loved ones coming home in aluminum caskets, an end to the casualties, an end to worry and heartbreak and a day of never-ending thanks.

All over the land—and peaceful, conservative Peterborough was no exception—ecstatic, joyful and thankful jubilation broke out. It was boundless.

Church bells and the Central School bell were pealing; volunteer firemen had the trucks out, going up and down Main and Grove Streets with lights flashing and sirens wailing. Everybody was downtown, laughing, singing and dancing in the streets, letting loose all the pent-up worry and anxiety that had built up during the past three years and eight months.

If one picture captured the mood and spirit of the day, it would have to be the photo, taken by Alfred Eisenstadt, of a sailor hugging and kissing a nurse in Times Square, which was on the cover of *Life* magazine. They were total strangers, but so what—the war was over!

Sergeant Jerry Kennedy, USMC

I couldn't have been more excited if it was Christmas morning when I was a little kid. Mom got a phone call. Cousin Jerry was coming to visit us for a few days. Jerry was Sergeant Jerome Kennedy, U.S. Marine Corps, and he was my hero. Like a lot of kids during World War II, we wrote to servicemen to cheer them up and show them our support for serving their country. It was the patriotic thing to do because they were keeping the Germans and Japanese from taking over our country. It was as simple as that.

Why I picked Jerry, I don't remember, because I had several cousins serving in the military, two of whom were killed in the line of duty. There was an eighteen-year difference in age between my mom and Jerry's dad, who had been a platoon leader in trench warfare during World War I with the Forty-second Infantry Division. World War I was supposed to have been the "war to end all wars."

Jerry was very faithful answering my letters, and I recall the thrill when, coming home from school, Mom would announce, "There's a letter to you from Jerry." Of course, I'd write him right back. Looking back, I'm sure it was an effort on his part to write to a kid cousin when he could have been on liberty call with his buddies.

It must have been toward the end of April 1945 when Jerry took the train from Cincinnati, Ohio, to Peterborough, New Hampshire, via Boston to visit us. He was with the Fourth Marine Division (FMF), Twenty-fourth Marines, and had just returned from the bloody, brutal and costly invasion and capture of Iwo Jima. The Third, Fourth and Fifth Marine Divisions had landed on Iwo Jima on February 19, 1945, and secured the island on March 26, 1945. Iwo Jima was Jerry's fifth campaign, so by now he was a battle-hardened U.S. Marine.

Prior to Iwo Jima, he was a veteran of landings in the Marshal Islands of Roi and Namur in January 1944 and the landing on Eniwetok Atoll in mid-February 1944. Next was the Marianas—Saipan in June 1944 and Tinian on July 24, 1944. It was on these landings that he'd been wounded several times. As I recall, he wore the Purple Heart ribbon with three clusters. He came off Iwo Jima with no injuries.

The tactical purpose of securing Saipan provided an air base for the B-29 Super Forts to bomb the Japanese homeland. Iwo Jima lay halfway between Saipan and Japan, so its capture denied the Japanese a base to launch fighter planes intercepting the B-29s on bombing runs. The airfield on Iwo Jima was also a haven for crippled B-29s returning from Japan. Strategically, Iwo Jima was vital, but it came at a horrific cost of six thousand marines killed and seventeen thousand wounded. The Japanese defenders lost their entire garrison of twenty thousand troops. Those not killed in combat committed hari-kari.

Looking back, I can't say Jerry's visit was exciting or entertaining for him, because Peterborough, New Hampshire, population twenty-five hundred, is a typical conservative small southern New Hampshire town—one movie hall, a bar and grill and a hotel that had been a stagecoach inn in years gone by. It is very possible that he enjoyed the peace and quiet of our town because he had had enough excitement to last several lifetimes. Of course, for me it was a most exciting occasion.

Up High Street, two doors from our place, was Mr. Fletcher Dole's village farm, consisting of seven Guernsey cows, a couple calves and two or three heifers. It was where I kept my Guernsey cow Vicki and her heifer, Roxy. On Saturday, I had barn chores to do, so I asked Jerry if he'd like to help, never giving a thought to what cow manure would do to his spit-shined, double-soled dress shoes and uniform.

"Well, cousin, I think I'll pass on that and take a walk downtown." Being a U.S. Marine and an Irishman, he somehow managed to find Gatto's Inn, the local watering hole. Gatto's was the unofficial headquarters of the 52-20 Club. Members of this "club" were returning World War II veterans who received twenty dollars for fifty-two weeks from the government while they were looking for employment and readjusting to civilian life. On the wall behind the bar were affixed unit designation patches of 52-20 veterans. Lo and behold, while there, Jerry met Donald "Blondie" Paquette, a U.S. Marine from the Fourth Division (FMF) who had also just come off Iwo Jima and was home on leave. Jerry and Blondie spent the remainder of the day and early evening swapping sea stories. Maybe they talked about the war; maybe they didn't.

I had the good sense never to ask Jerry about the war. I did, however, ask, "Did you see the Stars and Stripes raised on Mr. Suribachi?"

"You bet I did," Jerry said. "On February 24, five days after the initial landing, members of the Second Battalion, Twenty-eighth Marines, raised the colors. It was unbelievable but was by no means the end of the battle. We didn't secure Iwo until March 26, and by then we'd suffered thousands of casualties."

That was the only mention he made regarding the war. I recall, however, that he did make this observation: "Guys who beat their gums and chip their teeth telling war stories don't know what war really is."

On Monday morning, we put Jerry on the Boston and Maine (B&M) passenger train. Back in those days, every town, large and small, had a train station. I believe Peterborough ran one train, coming and going, per day. On March 17, 1953, at 2:05 p.m., the B&M train left the station for the last time.

Before boarding the train, Jerry stated matter-of-factly, "Well, the next operation is going to be a really tough one"—meaning, of course, the invasion of the Japanese homeland. We said our goodbyes, and Sergeant Jerome Kennedy, USMC, was gone. For several nights, I cried myself to sleep for fear that I'd never see Jerry again.

On August 6, 1945, the atomic bomb was dropped on Hiroshima, and the end of World War II was declared on August 14, 1945.

Sixty years after Jerry's visit, I fully realize what a kind, thoughtful and generous thing it was for him to do. He gave up leave time after being overseas for nearly three years to make a kid cousin very, very happy.

Agricultural Projects

Vicki

"But, Dad, when you were young, you had a pony!" That was the argument I always used when pushing for a Guernsey calf, something I wanted more than anything in the world.

My track record was not good when it came to staying interested in something for very long. That was why my dad didn't rush out and buy me a calf, particularly a real fancy one.

The idea of responsibility and the long-term commitment to care never entered my mind. All I wanted was a Guernsey calf of my very own. Looking back, I'm sure this concept did concern my dad—because animals are far different from toys—and explained why he was reluctant to buy me a calf.

With the exception of a few times when sick in bed, I never missed a day doing my chores, taking care of Vicki and, later, her offspring.

Finally, for my tenth birthday in 1942, Dad bought me a baby Guernsey calf. Her name was Victoria Ann of Old Town Farm. I called her Vicki, and she was the love of my life. She had a silky dark brown coat with a couple of white spots.

I kept her at a neighbor's barn, Mr. Dole's, on the edge of the village in New Hampshire and was ever faithful in taking care of Vicki. This proved to Dad that I could start a project and stick with it. In my eyes, she was the greatest Guernsey calf around. Looking back, however, I'll have to admit that she was on the common side.

About the middle of November 1943, Vicki came in heat. She was seventeen months old and weighed approximately 650 pounds; it was time she was bred. After school, Vicki and I headed for Mrs. Scott's Guernsey farm about three miles away to breed Vicki to their herd sire, Rosewald Boniface.

Two months later, Doc Tenney, our local veterinarian, examined Vicki via rectal palpitation for a pregnancy check. While doing so, he had this faraway look in his eyes, as if he were concentrating. "Yep, she's bred all right," he pronounced, "but she's carrying a bull calf. I can feel the ring in his nose!" He was dead serious. Was I ever disappointed! I wanted a heifer calf to raise, but what did I know? I was only an eleven-year-old kid, and Doc Tenney was an expert in the field of bovine reproduction.

Vicki was due to calve about the middle of August. On August 15, I found Vicki with her heifer calf! The next time I saw Doc Tenney, I informed him how wrong he had been. "Well" he countered, "I'm right half the time!" Can't argue that point.

On the way home with Vicki, we stopped at classmate Bob's house. For whatever reason, his mother, Marguerite, invited both Vicki and me into her kitchen, which was on ground level with the sidewalk. Marguerite wanted to see the new mother. After a short visit, Vicki and I turned around and went back out the door. Vicki was ever a lady and a polite guest.

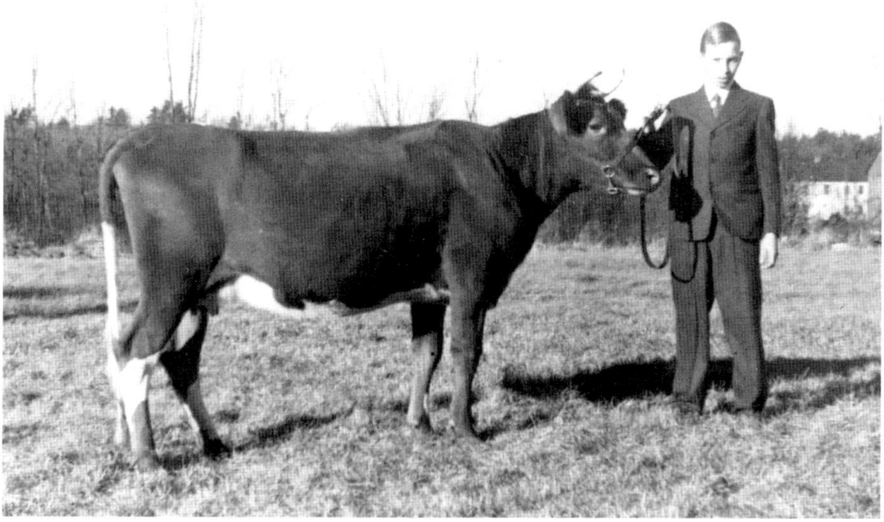

Tom Shultz and yearling Guernsey Vicki.

To further promote an interest in Guernsey cattle, my dad and the Hillsboro and Cheshire County 4-H Extension agents organized the Monadnock Calf Club. Club members were young kids in the Monadnock region interested in raising Guernsey calves, which we showed at the Cheshire County Fair. Some members would later develop Guernsey herds of their own. In March, a recognition banquet was held in Marlborough. Major A. Erland Goyette, from Peterborough, generously donated plaques and trophies to worthy recipients.

Gardens

Victory gardens were popular, patriotic and a necessity because canned goods were rationed during World War II.

Dad and I always had our garden planted by Memorial Day, a benchmark because in southern New Hampshire, the chance of a killing frost in early June was slim. Dad was fussy, so all rows were evenly spaced and straight, using a string as a guide.

Row crops, such as beans, peas, beets, etc., were planted two feet apart. Tomatoes were spaced in three-foot rows, with two feet between plants. Cabbage, broccoli and Brussels sprouts were spaced two feet apart in two-foot rows. Corn was planted with three kernels per hill, two feet apart in three-foot rows, which enabled me to cultivate the rows lengthwise and then cross-cultivate between the hills to control weeds.

Vine crops, such as cukes, squash and pumpkins, we planted at the garden's end, next to the corn in four-foot rows, with four feet between hills of three plants each.

After Dad helped me plant, controlling weeds was my job, using a sharp garden hoe and a high-wheel Kentucky cultivator. He built wooden tomato racks to keep the fruit off the ground and to make harvesting easier. I also think they ripened better with racks.

Harvesting was also my job, with some help from Mom, who, along with Grandma, did all the canning and preserving of vegetables, fruits, jam and jellies. Over the years, they must have put up hundreds of jars, and we continued raising a garden after the war because back then, home freezers were unheard-of.

Mr. and Mrs. Dole had a sizable garden each year. Sometimes crows would pull up the new sweet corn shoots to eat what was left of the seed corn. A product called "Crow Dope" was on the market, but it was a tar base and messy, fouling up our hand corn planter, so Mr. Dole had a simple solution to the crow problem: a grain dipper of cracked corn at the end of the patch. Crows are crafty birds, and they soon discovered that feasting on the cracked corn was a far better deal than pulling up plants for the remnants of seed corn.

Raccoons could be a problem, also. Just about the time the sweet corn ripened, they'd come in at night, pull down a stalk and eat the young corn. Mr. Dole designed and built a live trap to catch them, after which they were returned to the woods from whence they had come. This method was very successful.

One year during World War II, Dad and several of his friends, including me, planted a sizable potato patch down on Evans' Flats. At harvest time, they hired someone to come in with a mechanical potato digger, after which we picked the potatoes by hand, with everybody sharing in the bountiful yield. We dubbed ourselves the "Plucky Plow Boys"

Dad and I always raised a couple rows of carrots, which can be tiresome when it comes time to thin them out to allow room for each carrot to develop. We'd dig them up in the fall before the ground froze, put them into wooden boxes and cover them with moist sand. By keeping the sand damp, they kept very well through the winter.

Parsnips are also root vegetables, and they should be left in the ground all winter, until March, for a truly tasty vegetable. There's something about the frost in the ground that brings out the true parsnip flavor.

Poultry

During the war, I kept a flock of twenty-five New Hampshire Red hens, which laid over two hundred eggs per hen per year, so I had eggs to sell. I delivered them house-to-house. My neighbor, Mrs. Lenora Hunter, was kind enough to let me use her henhouse. Of course, these hens laid brown eggs; you couldn't give white eggs away in New Hampshire back then.

The agreement was that I supply Mom with eggs, but occasionally I'd come up short of eggs for my egg route, so I'd give her the cracked eggs instead. I was getting eighty-five cents a dozen for large eggs, delivered, and grain was $3.00 to $3.50 per hundred-pound bag.

I raised that rooster named Brigham. As he got older, he became feisty, coming at me with wings flapping and leg spurs clicking when I opened the henhouse door. He was guarding his harem, but I got tired of his behavior. One day when I opened the henhouse door, Brigham greeted me as usual, flapping his wings and clicking his spurs. That day, I was armed with a lightweight plaster lath, and I proceeded to dust his feathers. I didn't hit him hard, but just enough to scare him. We went round and round the henhouse, hens scattering in all directions. Apparently, he learned his lesson because he never bothered me again.

When winter arrived, my dad showed me a poultry management practice. "Just before dark," he advised, "feed them some laying mash mixed with warm milk diluted with water so when they roost at dark, they have fresh warm feed in their craws." Apparently, it was a good practice because twenty-five hens laid nineteen to twenty eggs daily all winter and into the spring. For whatever reason, he also had me add a few dashes of black pepper to their late-afternoon snack.

During another winter, I tried something different to feed my hens in the late afternoon so they would have a full craw before going to roost. My dad and I built wooden trays with screen bottoms that were placed in an upright rack that I kept in a warm cellar. I put ordinary grain oats in the trays and kept them watered, causing them to sprout so the hens could have some fresh, green herbage during the long New Hampshire winter months. Apparently, this, too, was successful because egg production held up very well.

During World War II, meat was rationed and scarce, so I raised capons, which are altered roosters. They grew fat and tender, and at about twelve to fourteen weeks, we dressed them for fryers or to be oven-roasted. My Grandma Kennedy took charge of the meat processing because she'd had experience as a farmer's wife out in Iowa.

How We Earned Money

Jobs

Back then, if there was something you wanted to buy or you needed spending money to take a girl to the movies and then get a snack at the Goodie Shop, you earned the money on your own. Not that what we earned was always spent because we also learned the value of saving. I had a savings account at the Peterborough Savings Bank when I was a kid. One time, they ran an ad in the *Peterborough Transcript* with a picture of me, proclaiming that I was one of their depositors. During World War II, Savings Bonds were a patriotic and economical way to save money because they paid a competitive rate of interest and were backed by the U.S. government. This was the major source of money to finance World War II.

The shadow of the recent Great Depression influenced our monetary values. Our parents had married and raised our generation during those times, so they knew the value of a dollar and expected us to do the same by earning our own money, saving a portion thereof and spending wisely.

If you wanted to work, there were readily available jobs, and there were no regulations regarding what an underage kid could or could not do because nobody really knew the definition of underage.

In the summer, there were lawns to mow, pushing a reel-type lawnmower by hand; they were power mowers, all right—powered by a kid. In the late 1940s, gas-powered mowers began to appear, but all the trimming along flower bed borders and trees was done by hand, using grass shears, thus reducing CO_2 emissions. Lawn mowers that were sharp and the shear bars set properly weren't all that hard to push, and mowing once a week kept the grass from becoming too high. In years of limited rainfall in late July and early August, once in ten days to two weeks was allowable. There was always garden and flowerbed work available, but other jobs took higher priority because the former was not the most popular.

Snow Shoveling

In the winter, snow was known as "white gold." Winter in Peterborough could begin in November and last until early March, but on average it lasted about three months. All the snow removal was done by hand—walkways and driveways, even parking lots. Snow blowers and pickup trucks with plows were unheard-of. The town Highway Department used trucks equipped with plows, and a small Caterpillar crawler with a blade plowed the sidewalks. After the snowfall, when all the roads and village streets had been cleaned, removing the snow banks on downtown streets was done by men shoveling snow into dump trucks, four to six men per truck. Front loaders mounted on tractors or conveyors weren't heard of, leastways not in Peterborough. The snow was hauled away and dumped into the Contoocook River, near the library bridge on lower Pine Street.

Frank, a World War II veteran, owned an old army 4x4 ambulance, ideal in snowy weather. He had agreements with a large number of residents, many of whom were Guernsey Club employees, to keep their walks and driveways clear of snow. This also included the Guernsey Club parking lot next to the GEM movie theater on School Street. Frank hired ten to a dozen guys to shovel snow, and being on his crew was a bonanza because he paid seventy-five cents an hour when forty cents was the going rate. We'd all crowd into the ambulance, which took us from job to job.

After a big snowstorm, we'd work way into the night because, one never knew, but it might snow again just as hard the next day. We provided our own shovels, which was fine because each guy had his personal preference of shovels. The shovels were waxed daily so that the snow would slide off easily, particularly if the snow was a tad tacky. It was hard work, but we were young, husky and needed the money. It was our first experience with federal income tax and Social Security withholding.

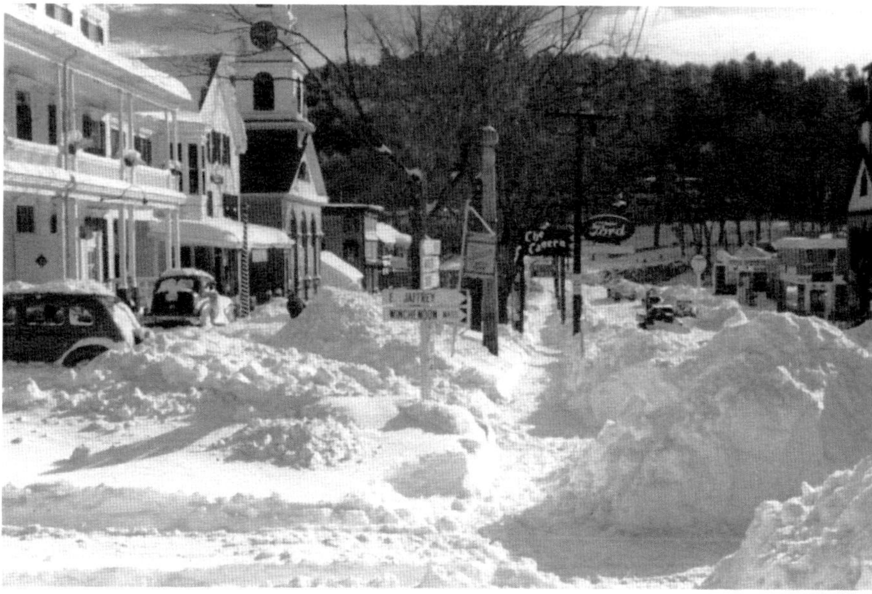

Snow: "white gold" for us guys to shovel and earn spending money. *Collection of the Peterborough Historical Society.*

As a kid, I got all excited with anticipation at the prospect of a big snowstorm, especially a nor'easter, for three reasons. First, it meant snow shoveling jobs; second, excellent skiing conditions at Whit's Ski Tow up at the Golf Club; and, last but not least, no school!

Fighting a Forest Fire

One fall in the late 1940s, the woods, undergrowth and forest floor were tinder dry because rainfall had been scarce during the preceding summer and early fall.

Conditions were just right for a major forest fire to break out, which it did over on Temple Mountain. We could see the fire's glare at night from our house on High Street in Peterborough. As I recall, Peterborough, Temple, Sharon and Jaffrey sent their volunteer fire companies to the scene, with back-up assistance from Greenville, New Ipswich, Wilton and South Lyneboro. The collective fire chiefs of each company and state forestry officials realized that a considerable amount of manpower would be needed to contain and control this conflagration. So the word went out. Would high school–age guys like to become forest fire fighters? Of course! There was a sense of excitement and adventure—and the prospect of making some serious money. The state Forestry Department agreed to pay us seventy-five cents an hour, but little did we know that forest fire fighting wasn't all excitement and glamour. It was bone-numbing hard work, not to mention dangerous.

Volunteer firemen are just that—they all had full-time jobs or owned business ventures. Some were fairly young men, and others not so young, so a prolonged forest fire would begin to take its toll. That's where us guys came in—we were young, tough and rugged, well suited to scrambling about the mountainous terrain with a pump tank of water weighing forty pounds strapped to our backs. We were assigned night duty. Gains the men made during the day were wiped out unless personnel could continue firefighting at night. The terrain was steep, rocky and rugged, covered with tinder-dry under growth that ignited larger trees. We were equipped with Smith Indian pump tanks, with a hand pump that squirted a sizeable stream of water, dousing flames and burning undergrowth.

Flames were everywhere, so running fire hoses up the mountain was both impractical and out of the question.

The fire chiefs worked out a system whereby 250-gallon stock tanks were spaced, one after another, up the mountainside. As I recall, there were five or six stations where we could refill our pump tanks.

Due to drought conditions, water had to be hauled in by tank trucks that pumped water up to water station #1, where a small portable gas water pump would supply water station #2, which in turn replenished other stations up the mountain side.

Army surplus walkie-talkies were used to communicate when each station needed more water. We'd fill our pump tanks, fan out wherever there was fire, empty our tanks on the flames and return to a water station for refilling. Thousands upon thousands of gallons of water were used to douse a stubborn fire, but after several days, the Temple Mountain forest fire was declared officially out.

Women's Auxiliary units from the volunteer fire companies and the Red Cross did a great job keeping us supplied with sandwiches, cookies and hot coffee. Food and drink were brought up the mountain, but occasionally we'd go down to where the makeshift kitchens were set up. One of my buddies,

Dick, stated in no uncertain terms, "I never want to see another cheese sandwich in my life!" This wasn't a complaint, just a statement of fact, because we were very thankful for any kind of sandwich, cheese or otherwise. I'm sure there were egg salad, peanut butter and jelly and bologna, too, but it was just our luck to get the cheese sandwiches.

My buddy Jerry had a close call. Just before dawn, when it was pitch black, he sat down to catch a couple winks of sleep. We were all bone tired by that time, so we'd get in short naps. When he woke in the pre-dawn hour, he noticed he was within one hundred feet of a chasm. Good thing he stopped when he did!

We didn't go to school that week, so during the day we slept and were back on the mountain at night. Mr. Gerald Faunce, our high school principal, never said a word. He understood the situation. All in all, it was an exciting adventure, and there was a sense of accomplishing a worthy goal—not to mention, the pay was great!

Dave Rockford, Peterborough Volunteer Fire Department chief, praised us: "If it hadn't been for those young guys fighting fire at night, I don't see how we could have contained that blaze."

Poultry Farm Work

During a couple of summers and on Saturdays during the winter, I worked at Nedlar Farms along with some other high school guys. Norman, Clint, Dick and Frankie are names that come to mind.

Nedlar Farms was engaged primarily in the hatchery business rather than producing eggs for the retail market. One of our major jobs was to make chick boxes and covers used to ship baby chicks by air to a grower in Georgia. We had a system whereby we made three hundred boxes and covers each Saturday during the year.

Nedlar Farms used an incubator that controlled temperature and humidity of the hatching eggs. Put another way, an incubator is a mechanical hen setting on her nest of eggs.

After the chicks hatch in twenty-one days, each incubator requires a thorough cleaning using an industrial vacuum cleaner. All the trays that housed the eggs until hatched were cleaned using a power washer. Both these tasks weren't our favorite jobs, but they paid forty cents per hour, good wages back then.

The Nedlar Farm flock didn't produce enough eggs to maintain the hatchery business, so smaller poultry men sold cases of hatching eggs to the farm.

Another one of our jobs was to place these eggs in trays that would then be put into the incubators. Nedlar Farms was an extensive poultry operation and employed a couple dozen people year round, plus us part timers.

Store Clerks

Two of my classmates, Bob and Fred, worked after school and on Saturdays as clerk and stock boys at two Peterborough grocery stores.

Bob worked at Walter Bryer's, a long-established merchant formerly known as Winch and Field. Mr. Bryer stocked the S.S. Pierce brand of canned goods, an up-scale product line favored by city folks who maintained summer homes in the vicinity of Peterborough. He also was one of the first to stock the Birdseye brand of frozen foods, and consequently, during his high school days, that was Bob's nickname.

Fred clerked and stocked shelves at the First National, a nationwide food store chain managed by Joe Robichaud. During World War II, rationing of canned goods was in effect, so the clerks had to deal with food ration stamps. They had to know which stamps and how many could be used between specific dates and for which rationed food items, so it could become confusing at times.

Back then, when you entered a retail grocery store, there was a center aisle, flanked on both sides by a wide counter. The produce display and meat department was generally at the rear of the store. Meat was delivered in halves, stored in a walk-in cooler and then carved into retail cuts by a butcher, a skilled craftsman in the meat business. Upon request, he would do some custom cutting. My uncle Harold Westover, who taught me deer hunting, was the butcher for many years at the Great Atlantic and Pacific Tea Co., better known then as the A&P.

Behind the counters, shelves stacked with all manner of grocery items reached to the ceiling. To reach items on the top shelf, the clerk used a long pole with a gripper attachment at the end.

By today's standards, the assortment of grocery goods was somewhat limited to customers, but I don't recall feeling put upon. Dry breakfast cereals were basic and did not contain added sugar. The brands I recall were

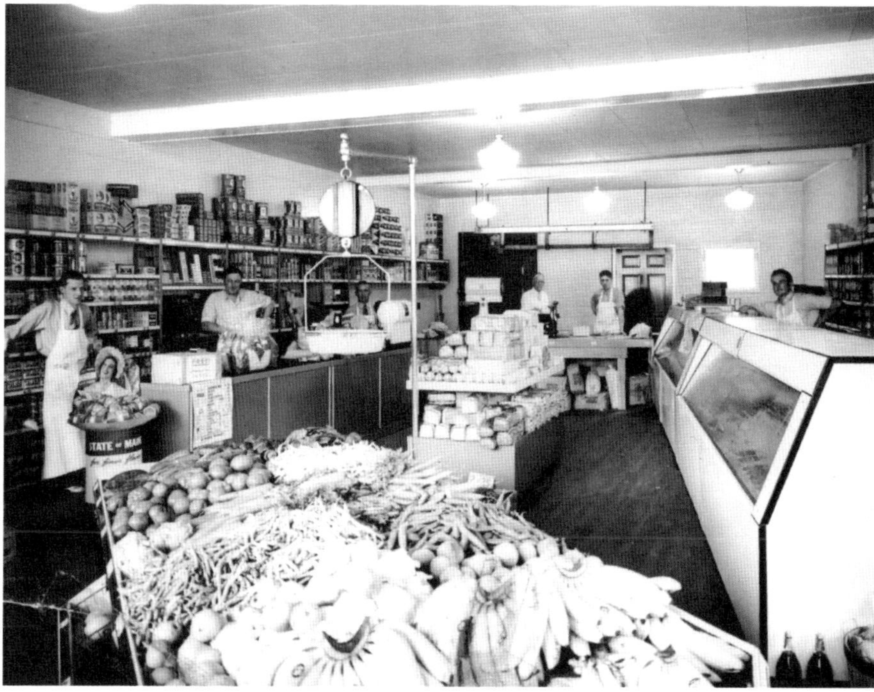

Wyman's Market. Note that clerks wait on customers; there was no self-service. *Collection of the Peterborough Historical Society.*

Corn Flakes, Wheaties, Rice Crispies, Puffed Wheat, Kix, Grape Nuts and Bran Flakes. Oatmeal, corn meal, Cream of Wheat and Ralston were our choices for cooked cereal.

You told the clerk what you wanted, and he placed your order in a bag; there was no self-service back then. He wrote a receipt, and you either paid the bill or it was put on a tab to be settled after payday.

During the Great Depression, it wasn't unusual for a merchant to grant extended credit to those who were down and out. Generally, he was eventually paid in full, but on occasion, he just wrote the bill off. The attitude then was that "we're all in this together," with the more fortunate ones helping out those who were on hard times. Better days were coming for everybody.

Bryer's store offered delivery service by customer request, so on Monday morning, Vernon Harris, a longtime employee, took grocery orders, which were put up back at the store in delivery baskets—which, incidentally, were made by the Peterborough Basket Company. Driving a Ford pickup truck with roof and side curtains, Mr. Harris made deliveries on Wednesday morning, and back then, ten dollars' worth of groceries would fill one of those baskets.

Back then, there was always work waiting to be done, so earning money for a savings account, to buy that special item or to take your girlfriend to the movies was just a matter of being ambitious.

Farm Work

Spring is the logical time of year to begin describing the yearly routine of farm work. Along about the last of April, when the ground had dried out and was no longer soft, it was time to clean out the winter's accumulation of cow manure in the barn cellar.

All our fieldwork was done with the help of Charlie, a bay Morgan gelding, middle aged, perhaps twenty to twenty-five years old. It was only natural that he be a Morgan because that was the Vermont farmer's breed of choice. Morgans were sturdy, rugged, of good disposition and could be ridden, driven in a carriage or do an honest day's work either in the field or woods.

Charlie was bred and raised by Mr. Dole's father-in-law, Luther Harrington, a Vermont farmer. Charlie was sound and had no bad habits. However, he was alert, and we kids were cautioned by Mr. Dole, "Don't chirp or cluck when around Charlie 'cause that's his signal to 'go,' and I want to be the one who tells him to 'go' for obvious safety reasons." You might say he was a tad fiery, in that he was always on the trot, even to the day he died, but he didn't have a mean bone in his body. Actually, Charlie did have one bad habit. When turned out to pasture with the cows, he would pull the shoes off his front feet, using a near hoof as a claw hammer. Of course, this meant a trip to the blacksmith, Mr. Downey, so Charlie had to stay in the barn when not working.

Since the early 1700s, New Hampshire barns were built with the cows facing the center barn floor, on each side of the barn, with a narrow walkway behind each row of stanchions. Loose hay was stored above the cow stable and on the scaffold above the center barn floor, where it was pitched into the cows' manger below. The cow beds were located on the second floor of the barn, allowing for a full cellar beneath. Behind the cow beds, there was a gutter with a trapdoor or scuttle about every four to six cows. When the gutters were cleaned night and morning, a person opened the scuttle and pushed the manure into the cellar below, then spread fresh dry sawdust on the cow beds to keep them dry and clean. By storing the manure, there wasn't the daily chore of spreading manure in deep snow, bitter cold or driving sleet and rain. Environmentally, it was also sound practice to wait until spring to spread the manure until after the snow had melted, particularly on hilly meadows.

Twentieth-century dairy farmers have abandoned the old-fashioned barns and are using several manure storage facilities that accomplish the same goal, but with a higher price tag. Maybe the New Hampshire dairy farmers were two hundred years ahead of their time!

At any rate, back to spring's farm work. Hitched to the manure wagon, Charlie would back it under the barn, where Mr. Dole, his hired school lad Maurice and I loaded the manure into the wagon with dung forks and then spread it on hay meadows and gardens. Mr. Dole believed that a good coat of cow manure was the difference between a great and just an average garden, yielding tasty and nutritious vegetables. Some farmers used ground-driven manure spreaders, but they required a team of horses to operate, and Charlie was our lone horse. The same could be said for plowing, which required a team pulling a single moldboard plow. The Murray brothers were teamsters and owned several pairs of workhorses, so they did the plowing in and around Peterborough.

Of course, it was hard work to spread the load by hand, but we didn't feel misused; it was just the way things were, and we got the job done.

Mr. Dole's cropping system was no frills, yet economical and practical. He didn't grow corn for silage, nor do I recall him ever plowing a field to be reseeded to alfalfa and timothy. Some of the better hay meadows received a coating of cow manure each spring. One fall, we cleaned poultry range shelters at Nedlar Farms, hauling the chicken manure and spreading it by hand on a hay meadow at the MacDowell Colony. He harvested whatever local hay meadows offered, which was mostly orchard grass and timothy. There were large hay meadows at the MacDowell Colony, where we harvested most of the winter's supply of hay. This worked well because the management at the colony wanted to keep these meadows open; otherwise, the woods would reclaim them as they had been two hundred years ago. Some years, when there was an abundance of hay, we stored it in the barn at Hillcrest, the original farm at the colony. During the winter, we hauled it to Mr. Dole's barn with the aid of George Starkweather's one-ton platform body Chevy truck.

Mr. Dole knew that late-cut hay wasn't the best of quality, so he supplemented the ration with citrus and beet pulp, both of which were good sources of energy and protein and priced right. I used to snack on the citrus pulp; it was quite tasty. Beet pulp isn't succulent by any stretch of the imagination, but after Mr. Dole soaked it in hot water and mixed in some blackstrap molasses, it was transformed into a treat for both the cows and me. He was also generous with the grain scoop: "The eye of the master fattens his cattle."

Before we started making hay, we got our equipment ready. The wagon box was lifted off the running gear and replaced by the hayrack. Mr. Dole packed the running gear wheel hubs with grease; we took the cutter bar out of the horse-drawn mowing machine, replaced any knives and tightened loose rivets. I would turn the grindstone while Mr. Dole sharpened the knife sections. He applied grease to fittings and checked the gearbox oil level. Now we were ready to start haying, which would last all of July and part of August.

Mr. Dole began making hay after the Fourth of July, weather permitting—a general rule of thumb back then. By that date, the hay crop had reached its maximum growth for a first cutting and allowed for a second-cutting harvest toward the end of August. All of his hay was orchard grass and timothy.

When the weather looked promising, with several days of sunshine forecast, Mr. Dole hitched Charlie to the McCormick-Deering one-horse mowing machine with a five-foot cutter bar and began putting down hay.

After the hay was mowed, it took at least two days to cure; then it was raked into windrows with a dump rake, and the windrows were forked into large stacks.

Several of us neighborhood kids helped with haying, and our main job was to "tread hay" so Mr. Dole could put on a full load. We weren't big enough to pitch hay—that was the task of one of Mr. Dole's hired high school lads and Johnny, a young fellow from the village who helped with haying.

Jabbing the fork into a pile of hay, I watched in awe as Johnny lifted the hay upward and onto the hayrack in one smooth, fluid motion, causing the hardwood fork handle to actually bend—or at least so it seemed.

Mr. Dole's job was to place hay on the hayrack, putting a forkful on each of the four corners first and then filling in the sides, front and end. He always kept the corners higher so the middle of the load was at a lower level, which prevented the load from sliding off the hayrack. One of the neighbor kids, Judy, got pretty good at placing hay on the load.

One of my jobs was to run the bull rake, also known as a loafer, an ingenious tool with eight or ten curved teeth, each three feet long. After getting the knack of handling this tool, invented a couple hundred years ago, it was a smooth and efficient way to pick up the scatterings. One had to be clever and quick or those teeth would nip your heels, and they could get caught on a hummock of grass. Hay growing close to trees or stonewalls was cut with a snath and scythe and later gathered with the bull rake.

After the hayrack was full, we'd head to the barn, all of us kids riding on top of the load. From atop the load, Charlie looked so small, but he was up to the task of pulling the hayrack, which actually wasn't very heavy.

At the barn, the hay was unloaded the same way it was loaded—by hand, as Mr. Dole didn't have a horse-powered hayfork. Again, we kids were up in the mow, treading hay to keep it packed down. It was hot and dusty, but we were learning the value of work and how to be useful. There's nothing wrong with that, and it was a badge of honor to help with every single load of hay, every day.

Haying usually lasted until the end of July, and rainy days put a stop to haymaking. Should there be hay down, partly dry, and it got rained on, we turned each and every windrow over by hand with a pitchfork, then it took another good drying day or two. Mr. Dole didn't want any damp hay going into the barn, which would mean moldy and dusty forage. The worst scenario involving wet hay is spontaneous combustion and a resulting barn fire; once a barn catches fire, seldom is it ever saved.

Along about the middle of August, we harvested rowen off the better meadows. *Rowen* is a Norman-French term for "aftermath" or "second-cutting grass hay." Because the days were getting shorter and the sun's rays weren't as hot, it took at least three days to cure rowen, and for us kids, summer vacation was just about over.

Late summer was the time of year to get in bedding for the winter ahead. There was a sawmill down at the North Village, which probably began operations to saw out logs blown down by the 1938 hurricane. There were several huge piles of sawdust. The top couple inches of sawdust had dried during the summer, so we used old-fashioned wooden rakes, turned upside down, to rake the dry sawdust into windrows. Using a scoop shovel, we filled burlap bags, loaded them onto Charlie's wagon and drew them home, where they were stored in a shed, to be used that winter to bed the cows, keeping them dry and clean.

Later in the fall, after the maple trees had shed their leaves and before it rained, we bagged them up in large burlap bags for use as bedding for the calves and young cattle during the winter.

Another fall task, after the first killing frost, was cutting sweet corn stalks, which were fed to the cows during their last days on pasture. Most all the neighbors raised sweet corn, and they were glad to get rid of the stalks. We used the hayrack to get them home, where they were piled against a stone wall near the pasture. Each night, the cows got a couple of bundles to snack on during the night.

In the late fall, it was time to bank the house with leaves to keep out the winter wind and cold. As I recall, a roll of tar paper was tucked against the side of the house. Mr. Dole drove stakes in the ground one and a half or two feet away from the house foundation and then nailed lengths of slab wood on the inside of the stakes, probably two feet high. This inner space was filled with leaves and packed so as to eliminate air spaces, which kept the icy fingers of winter from probing into the cellar. When spring arrived, the process was reversed, and we took the leaves to a compost pile enclosed on three sides by a slab wood wall. Mrs. Dole used this compost for the various flower beds she maintained around the house.

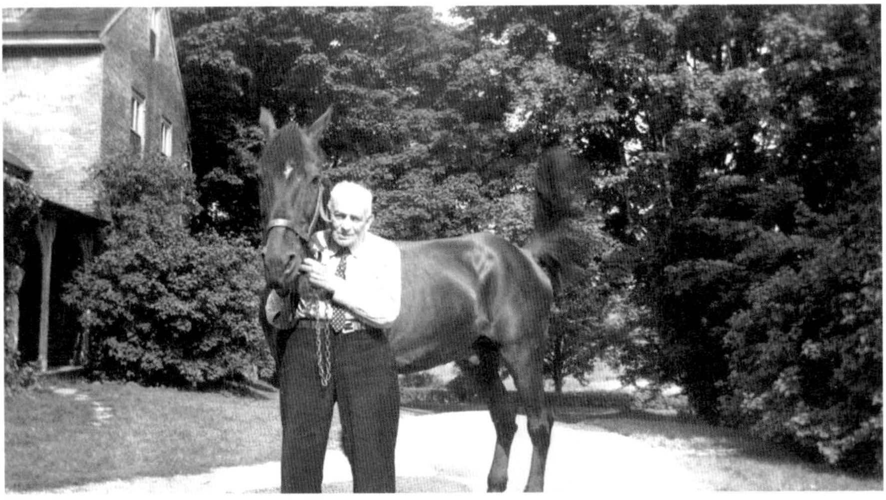

Charlie and Mr. Dole's father-in-law, Luther Harrington. *Courtesy of Dotty Dole Johnson.*

As you have noticed, there was little mechanization on the Dole Farm, and with the exception of Charlie, the mowing machine, the hay rake and hayrack, most of the farm work was done by hand. We didn't feel ill used because that was the way farms operated back then. We kids did master a valuable lesson; we learned how to work, to begin a task and follow it through to its successful completion, thus reaping the rewards of a job well done. Mr. Dole believed that honest work was a way of life, something to be proud of.

Charlie's Last Load

Everybody in Peterborough knew Charlie, Mr. Dole's bay Morgan gelding. They knew him by the rhythmic, staccato sound of hooves on pavement as he hauled hayracks piled high with fragrant grass hay for the seven purebred Guernsey cows on Mr. Dole's small High Street farm. His black forelock, mane and tail streamed in the wind as he trotted about his work. Always on the trot, it wasn't his nature to walk or plod the way other draft horses moved. Mr. Dole had long since learned that it was futile trying to hold Charlie to a walk.

It was one of those crisp days in August with a hint of fall in the air when cirrus clouds ride the clear blue sky and, for school kids, when their days of freedom are numbered because fall term would begin in a few days.

Mr. Dole and I were finishing a cutting of rowen at McDowell Colony. In the days before blacktop, the McDowell road was sand, and Charlie's hooves raised puffs of dust, trotting as usual, pulling an empty hayrack. Just past the Seccombe place, the road rises sharply and bends to the left. Near the crest, Charlie stumbled a step or two. I noticed that Mr. Dole was concerned—Charlie never, ever faltered. But he picked up the pace for thirty or forty yards. Just beyond the crest, he went down in a heap between the wagon shafts.

We both bailed off the hayrack. "Hold his head, Tommy, so's he doesn't thrash and hurt himself!"

Mr. Dole unhitched the trace chains and pushed the wagon backward. Poor Charlie made a feeble effort to get up, the whites of his eyes showing his terror, and I cradled his head as best I could. His soft velvety muzzle was warm against my bare arm, but in an instant, the muscles in his powerful body gave a shudder, and his hind legs tried a few feeble kicks. Exhaling, his last breath came out with a rattling sound and, in an instant, Charlie went limp. Mr. Dole was solemn as he bent over and lifted an eyelid. Eyes that once were lively and alert stared blankly at an afternoon that no longer was bright and clear.

"Charlie's drawed his last load of hay," Mr. Dole proclaimed. "Probably the old ticker just plain gave out." Stoic and not one to show emotion, I'm sure he felt sad and was torn up inside. They'd spent so many years working together to provide a living for Mr. Dole's family. All the good times the three of us had enjoyed—and it ended like this? It was my first experience seeing an animal die, never thinking that they don't live forever, but many years later, as a dairy farmer, I learned a sad truth about livestock: they all go through that barn door for the last time, one way or another.

Having been a farmer all his life, Mr. Dole had learned this sad fact about the fate of all livestock—that the good times don't last forever. He accepted Charlie's death as such, which explained his outward lack of emotion.

Charlie was becoming cold and stiff. Kneeling beside him, I remembered the good days of his life. He and Mr. Dole had harvested the hay on small meadows scattered about the neighborhood and on the larger fields at the colony. Every spring spent spreading the manure from the cellar under the barn on hay meadows and neighbors' gardens. Without Charlie, none of these jobs could have been accomplished. Charlie took it easy in the winter. On occasion, Mr. Dole would take him out on a lunge rope so Charlie could roll in the snow. He would get on his back, roll back and forth and then spring spread-legged to his feet, whinnying with horsey delight, shaking sheets of snow off his heavy winter coat and running at a full gallop in circles.

Charlie enjoyed life, and his wants were simple—a pail of water, a measure of grain, forkfuls of hay, a clean dry stall and work to do so as to be useful. The care and attention of his master was also important.

These were precious memories of the past, but now we had to deal with the present in giving Charlie a proper burial. With the help of some local husky lads, we loaded Charlie onto George Starkweather's stake rack Chevy truck and took him to the Moore Farm in South Peterborough. Here, the soil was sandy, and digging a grave was easy. Even so, it takes a big hole to bury a horse. "I want Charlie laid in the ground natural-like," Mr. Dole commanded. His legs were straight, his head and neck were flat and his black tail lay beside his lifeless body. Viewing him from above, he appeared to be trotting. In life, he was always on the trot, so why not in death?

Mr. Dole didn't buy another horse until the following spring because we had no need for one during the winter. Come spring, it was time to haul out the cow manure stored during the winter in the barn cellar.

Mr. Titcomb, a dealer in cattle and horses, sold Mr. Dole a middle-aged, pure white gelding, sound and supposedly clever and handy. "What shall we call him?" queried Mr. Dole. Immediately, I came up with an original name: Snowball. One warm, sunny Saturday in late April, after the snow had gone from the hay meadows, we harnessed Snowball to the manure wagon, intending to do a good days' work cleaning out the barn cellar. Snowball paid not a whit of attention to any of Mr. Dole's commands, standing stock still, solemnly observing the scenery and switching his tail at a horsefly or two. Mr. Dole wasted no time in making a phone call to Mr. Titcomb. "That horse you sold me is dumb as a post and crow bait to boot," protested Mr. Dole. "Bring me a horse I can use!"

Mr. Titcomb was both surprised and taken aback. He defended Snowball. "That's mighty strange," he declared. "That horse has been used the past six or eight years logging in northern New Hampshire. His French-Canadian teamster, a man of his word, gave the horse a good reference; he traded with me because he needed a younger horse."

That explained why Snowball didn't understand Mr. Dole's commands. "It will be a lot easier to teach Snowball English than for me to learn French!" vowed Mr. Dole, and sure enough, Snowball proved to be both clever and handy, and he learned all the English he needed to know.

Winter Sports

Sledding

During the winter, sledding was a popular pastime after school or on Saturdays. We'd go up to Mr. Dole's cow pasture, which had some steep slopes that made for fast sledding. Back then, our sleds weren't motorized like the twenty-first-century variety. They had two steel runners, a wood platform on which to lay or sit and two handles used for steering. You steered by pulling the handles right or left, which twisted the front of the runners in those directions. Also, by dragging the right or left toe of your snow boot, you could further aid in steering.

We'd hold our sleds while taking several running steps, drop the sleds to the ground and then flop on top in order to get up instant starting speed. It worked every time. After reaching the bottom of the hill, you pulled your sled back to the hilltop using a rope hooked to the steering handles.

A favorite sledding game was "follow the leader." Each of us guys took turns being the leader, who could go wherever he dared to go and the rest of us had to follow close behind him. Each leader tried to outdo the previous one by picking a trickier trail to follow—around trees, over natural-made jumps or just plain straight downhill.

One Christmas, my mom and dad gave me a Flexible Flyer sled; they were the BMWs of sleds and came in several different models. Mine happened to be a model with high clearance underneath, which enabled me to go in deeper snow. It was also a long sled, so when lying flat, my feet just barely hung out over the end (we always lay facedown rather than sitting upright).

Of course, after a downhill run, you had to pull your sled back to the top, which partially explains why there were few fat kids among us. Another reason might be that there were no fast-food outlets, and you ate three balanced meals at home. We didn't even have a school cafeteria.

As we were trudging back up the hill one afternoon, I noticed a tree stump sticking above the snow surface. I mentally asked myself, "Could my sled clear that stump?" Sure enough, it cleared, just barely. When it came my turn to be the leader, I picked a daring course that wove around huge pine trees, over a rock ledge and finally over that stump. By now, our sleds had picked up some speed, and I sailed over the stump. Looking over my shoulder, I noticed that the kid following was right behind me—minus his sled, which had come to a screeching halt when it didn't clear that stump.

Skiing

We moved to New Hampshire from Iowa in November 1937. Living in New Hampshire, it was natural that I take up skiing. Both New Hampshire and Vermont are famous for the number and quality of their ski areas and abundant snowfall. The Stowe, Vermont Chamber of Commerce slogan proclaims, "There's always snow, you know, at Stowe," where the Mount Mansfield ski area is located.

That first winter, one of my dad's business associates, Mr. Elsworth Bunce, gave me my first ski lessons. In his younger days, he had been a pretty fair skier. I called him Uncle Al because saying "Mr. Bunce" was formal, and referring to him as Al or Elsworth was out of the question. Kids never called an adult by their first name; this was considered disrespectful and rude.

My first lessons took place on a gentle slope at his house, and my first skis were wood, equipped with only a toe strap. The poles were bamboo.

The very first lesson Uncle Al taught me was how to fall down correctly. Believe it or not, there is a right way and a wrong way to fall down. As you learn to ski, falling down comes with the territory; however, as you become more proficient, you tend to fall down less and less. His instructions were: When you know for certain that you've lost your balance and that you're going down, don't fight it! Go down on one side or the other, never backward.

Keep your arms above your head, your knees slightly bent, get your body relaxed and stretched out and never allow yourself to get curled up into a ball. Don't sit back on your skis because this creates a runaway toboggan with you as the only passenger, headed for another skier, tree or stone wall. Some of the other basics Uncle Al taught were how to stop, snowplow to slow down and turn right and left. This was before rope tows and chair lifts, so I learned how to climb back up the hill with skis attached, using the herringbone technique. Uncle Al taught me well because in the following twenty-five years, I skied at areas all over Vermont and New Hampshire and never broke a bone or suffered a sprain.

As I got better and better at skiing, I used more elaborate ski bindings and skis. The first big improvement was a metal toe plate and leather bindings; then came cable bindings, steel edges on the skis and, finally, a cable binding with a safety release for the skis. One of the major causes of broken legs while skiing is that, upon a fall, the skis act as levers, twisting your legs as you spin. At a given pressure, the binding releases your foot from the skis, and a toggle strap hooked to both the ski and ski boot prevents a runaway ski from going down the slope—a great danger to other skiers below.

In the late 1930s and early 1940s, Howard Whitcomb established a ski slope at the Peterborough Golf Club on upper High Street. The first year or two, there wasn't a rope tow, but the ski enthusiasts from far and near gathered on weekends to ski down the slope, using the herringbone maneuver to climb back to the top of the hill. We did this all afternoon and considered it great fun. Peterborough had a reputation for ample snowfall to form a base, with additional snowfall for a packed powder surface. Artificial snowmaking was unheard-of.

In the 1920s, Woodstock, Vermont, claimed the first rope ski tow, and by 1946, there were one thousand ski tows, lifts and cable cars in the United States. Conveyances that returned skiers from the bottom of a slope to the top, safely and with ease, were a tremendous boon to the ski industry. They greatly increased the actual downhill skiing time that would otherwise be used in climbing back to the top.

Howard owned a small construction company. He was a visionary and recognized that the ski industry offered economic opportunities and would provide jobs for his crew during the off-season.

As Peterborough became a popular ski area, Howard expanded the ski facilities by making longer trails. He and his crew were innovative, good

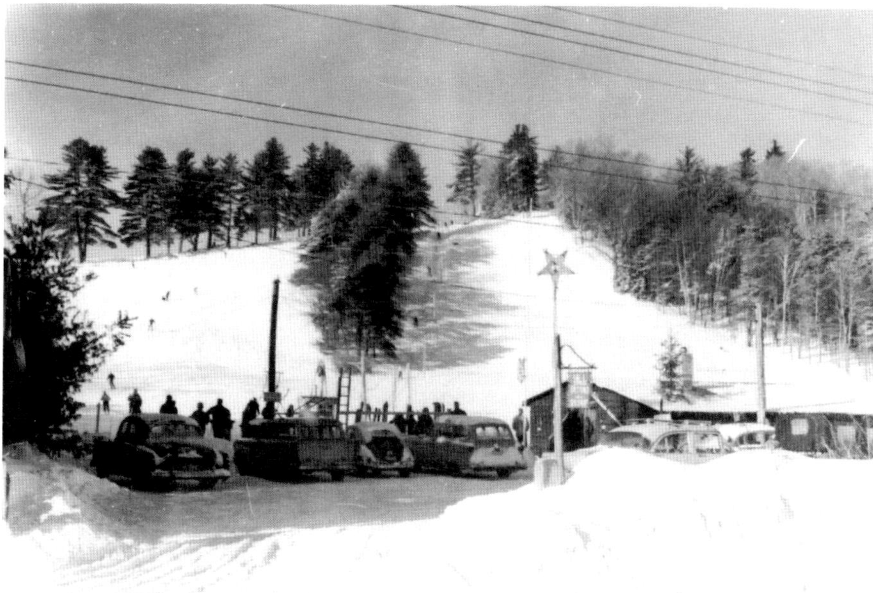

Whit's ski tow, Peterborough, New Hampshire. *Collection of the Peterborough Historical Society.*

mechanics and had Yankee ingenuity. At the top of the ski slope, they positioned a Model A Ford in what we called the "tow house." The Ford was jacked up and placed on blocks, and the tire was removed from the rear rim. A rope, about an inch in diameter, was laid on the uphill slope, run through a heavy overhead pulley at the tow house and then strung around the rear tire rim. Through a series of overhead pulleys, attached to tall poles above the skiers' heads, the rope returned back down the slope. At the bottom of the slope it ran through a sturdy and well-anchored pulley, starting back up the slope in a direct line to the tow house.

At a given distance from the tow house, a "crash gate" was built. Attached to the gate was a cable, connected to an engine shut-off switch on the Model A. This was a safety feature that prevented skiers from getting too close to the tow house and the resulting vicious twist of the towrope.

One of Howard's crew, usually it was Starr Sumner, was in the tow house making sure everything was running safe and sound.

It took a while to acquire the knack of how much and how fast to grab the rope as it moved uphill. Grab it quickly and you'd be jerked off your feet, or apply insufficient pressure and you'd go nowhere fast. Very soon, two deep tracks would be worn into the snow as more and more skiers ascended the slope. Just hang on tight and enjoy the ride, remembering the days when you climbed back up the slope on your own.

The afternoon was bright and sunny, with perfect snow conditions, and the weather was brisk but not windy or bitter cold. I had the towrope tucked under both arms as I approached the let-off point. Someone at sometime had skied into the crash gate, causing it to break, so we were getting the tow much closer to the tow house than normal.

Someone who understands the principles of physics can explain why the rope develops a wicked spin as it approaches the tow house. I was unaware that my ski parka was being literally wrapped up in the rope. When I tried to let go of the rope, I couldn't. "No problem," I thought to myself, "I'll just pull myself out of the parka." But this didn't happen because the parka cuffs were held tight about my wrists. I was getting closer and closer to the tow house, and now the rope was making a sharp incline as it approached a set of pulleys. I was held fast to the rope, and my skis were starting to leave the ground. Fortunately, Starr Sumner was paying attention and, noticing a very bad situation developing, was quick to shut down the Model A engine.

Had it not been for his swift reaction, I'd be writing this story with artificial hands. I am forever grateful to Starr Sumner, and may he rest in peace.

The crash gate was fixed and restored immediately, and despite the scare, I kept on skiing for the remainder of the day.

As the sun began to sink behind Mount Monadnock and the shadows lengthened, Starr announced, "This is the last run for today, folks; we're shutting down 'til tomorrow."

There's no doubt that all through high school and later at college, skiing was my favorite sport. I spent as much time as possible on the ski slopes of Peterborough and later throughout New Hampshire and Vermont.

One Christmas vacation, Billy, Tom and I journeyed up to Mount Mansfield, located near Stowe, Vermont. Even though it was the third week of December, there was very little ski activity in New Hampshire due to lack of snow, which was very unusual for that time of year.

We packed camping gear, food and our ski equipment in Bill's car, with the idea of camping out at the ski area, which was a common practice for kids on Christmas vacation. As we drove farther and farther north through New Hampshire, snow was scarce to nonexistent, and we began having second thoughts about our trip. But lo and behold, as we got nearer and nearer to

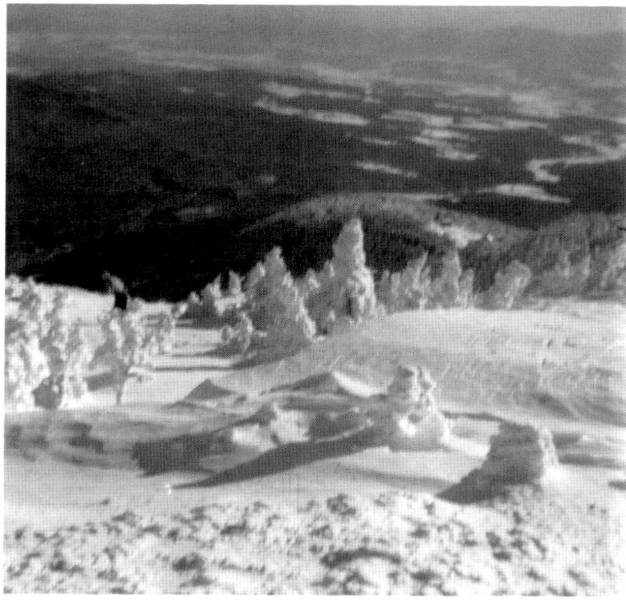

View of Mount Mansfield, Stowe, Vermont, from the chair lift. *Courtesy of Tom Day.*

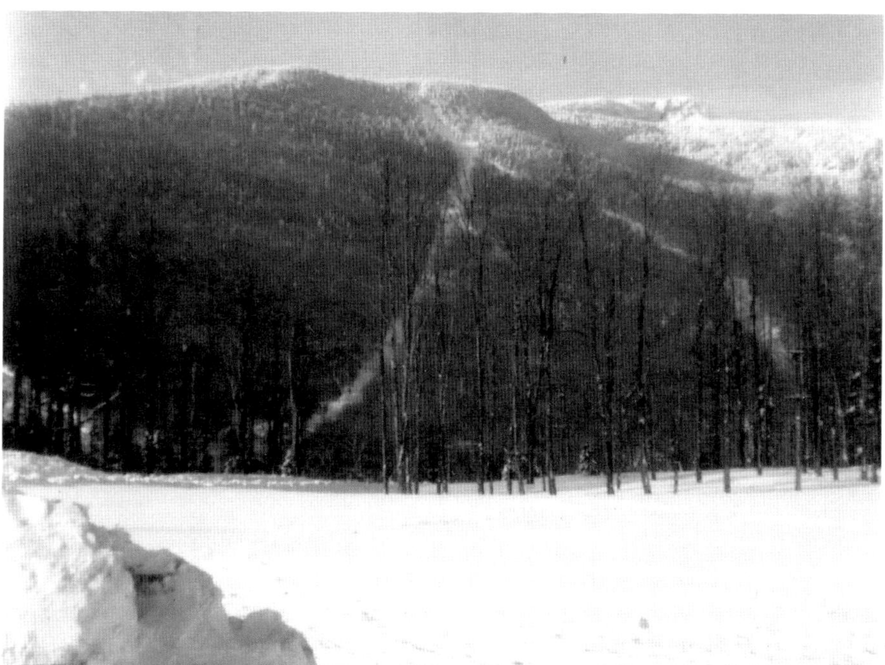

One of many ski trails on Mount Mansfield, Stow, Vermont. *Courtesy of Tom Day.*

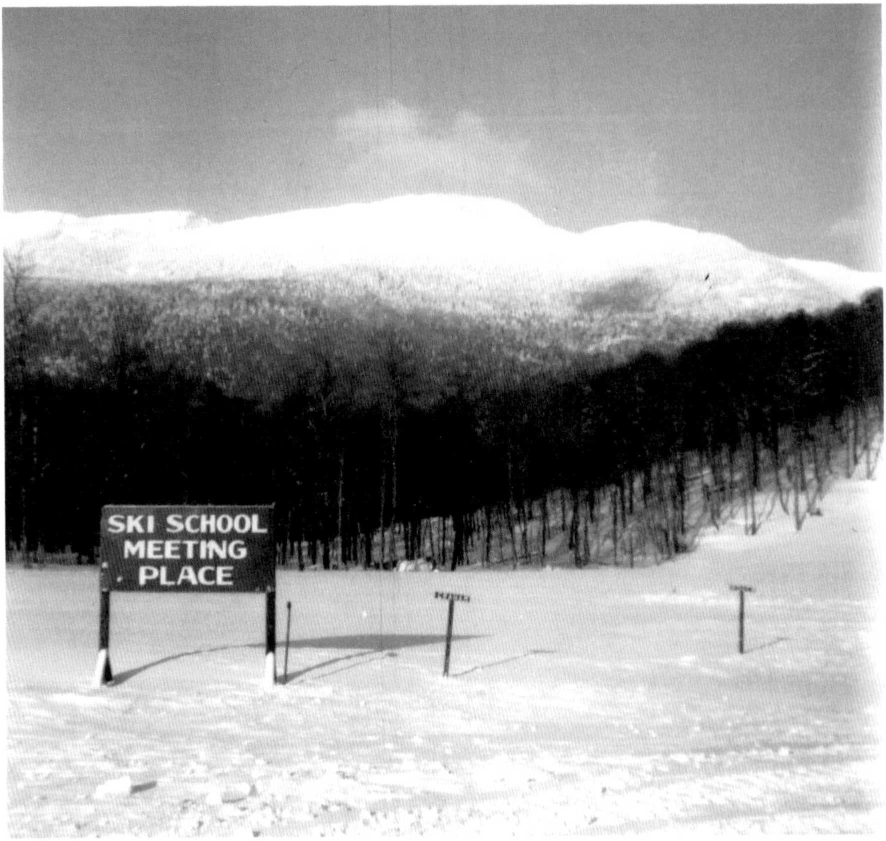

Mount Mansfield. *Courtesy of Tom Day.*

Stowe, we began seeing snow. We arrived at Mount Mansfield to find two to three feet of snow base; that night, it snowed another foot, creating a perfect packed-powder surface. The weather cleared and it turned bitter cold, but we had excellent skiing. All the chair lifts were supplied with bear and buffalo skin robes to ward off the cold. Once you started down one of a dozen trails, you were no longer cold because there was plenty of exertion to keep you warm.

Having enjoyed hundreds of happy and thrilling days rocketing down the ski slopes of Vermont and New Hampshire, I'm forever grateful that my dad chose to settle his family in Peterborough.

Tobogganing

Mr. Elsworth Bunce, known to me as "Uncle Al," was an organizer and an idea man, which explains why he was head of the Promotion Department at the American Guernsey Cattle Club, headquartered in Peterborough.

He thought it would be a good idea to organize a club to promote winter sports, resulting in the Peterborough Recreation Club (PRC), annual dues being one dollar.

One of the club projects was maintaining the toboggan tower, chute and runway at the Peterborough Golf Club. If my guess is right, it probably was built by the CCC during the Great Depression from timber logged after the 1938 hurricane. The tower was a high structure, probably forty or fifty feet tall. Climbing to the top was accomplished by a set of switchback stairs, flanked by a trough so you could pull the toboggan to the top of the tower. At the top of the tower was the launching chute, a box-like structure where the toboggan was placed and riders climbed aboard. Ahead of the launch chute was the runway, a very steep decline as it came off the tower and then gradually leveled off as it traversed one of the golf course fairways. The runway was just a bit wider than a toboggan and had wooden sides about a foot in height. It probably was a quarter mile in length and ended on a trail through the woods, where the toboggan finally coasted to a stop.

Packed snow and ice covered both the chute and runway, and when the temperature dipped below the freezing point, a volunteer group of young lads used a fire hose and water to keep the surface frozen, slippery and fast.

A toboggan held eight to ten passengers, packed like sardines in a can to ensure that nobody fell off. That would have been a disaster! A rope was attached to both sides of the toboggan, enabling the passengers to hang on for dear life. You grabbed the rope with your knuckles always inboard because initially the toboggan yawed side to side coming down the runway.

Four husky lads manned the chute, two on each side. After everybody was packed in the toboggan, they lifted the rear of the chute, which was hinged at the front, about four or five feet high, and you were on the way for the ride of your life. Accelerating from zero to forty miles per hour in less than ten seconds brought forth yells and screams of delight—with maybe a little fear mixed in!

It was some thrill for those in the front of the toboggan leaving the chute to look down that glassy, ice-covered runway, illuminated at night, and feel the icy wind whipping past your face.

Time has dimmed my memory, so I don't remember all the young Peterborough lads who volunteered their time so that we could enjoy some winter fun, but a few come to mind: Blondy and Lee, Richard, Freddie, Joe and Larry. After Pearl Harbor, they all went off to war.

I would estimate that the entire run was about a quarter mile, so it was quite a walk back to the tower pulling your toboggan. After a few runs, you'd become tired, hungry and cold, especially on subfreezing nights, so a stop at the warming hut was in order. A chunk wood stove threw off lots of heat, and hot chocolate and doughnuts took care of the hunger, after which you were ready for more tobogganing.

Skating Rink

Another PRC project was a skating rink on what had been the grounds of the old Phoenix Factory. Now it is the site of the American Guernsey Cattle Club building. Members of the Peterborough Volunteer Fire Department kept the rink surface smooth, and us guys cleared the snow with shovels, scrapers and brooms after a storm. There was a warming hut where you could lace your skates, and skating music from a 78rpm record player with speakers added to the fun on many cold and wintry nights.

Class Trip

During the spring vacation at Easter time, the class of 1950 Peterborough High School embarked on our class trip to Washington, D.C. We had spent a lot of time organizing and working on various fundraising projects to finance the trip, and as I recall, we put some of our own earnings into the kitty. I am sure that our parents, relatives, friends and people we hardly knew were glad when the fundraisers were over, because they had all had enough baked goods, magazine subscriptions and greeting cards to last a lifetime—maybe even two.

When we left Peterborough, snow banks were fighting a losing battle against several days of temperatures in the fifties. However, arriving in Washington, we were greeted by cherry blossoms, daffodils and tulips in bloom along the Potomac River

Forty-two seniors left Peterborough on a bright sunny Monday morning on the Granite Stage bus bound for Boston, where we boarded a train for the remainder of the trip. The Granite Stage was owned by the dad of classmate Donnie Myhaver, and our driver for the trip was Roy Robbins, uncle of classmate Richard Robbins. Back then, train travel was reliable; they ran on schedule, the coaches were clean and the food in the dining car, including the service, was excellent. And equally as important, it was affordable.

Our chaperones were Mr. and Mrs. Arnold Barker, a high-school-kid-friendly couple. Several of us seniors used to hang out at their place on Windy Row, and for that reason, we called Mrs. Barker "Ma."

I don't recall any pre-trip lectures on what we could and couldn't do or what we should and should not do, and there was no searching of luggage for booze or drugs. In the 1940s, drinking or drugs weren't part of the scene. Minors couldn't buy alcohol, and no adult was about to buy it for us. Stealing it from our parents' liquor cabinet was a bad option as well. I do recall one occasion where, somehow, three or four of us guys acquired a quart of Narraganset Ale, and we polished it off. We fancied ourselves as two-fisted drinkers; however, there was not a repeat performance. Our exposure to drugs was limited to scenes from a movie where an opium den and water pipes were depicted somewhere in another part of the world. Street drugs and illicit use of prescription drugs were unheard-of.

Apparently, it was a given that we were responsible and grown-up and would behave accordingly. In two months, we would graduate, entering the outside world. If we hadn't learned by now how to conduct ourselves as adults, it was too late at this point.

Our first stop was New York City—a first for most of us. That evening we saw the Rockettes perform the traditional Easter show, followed by a feature movie at Radio City Music Hall. We had seats down front. The Empire State Building, Rockefeller Center, the Statue of Liberty, Central Park, Times Square and maybe a museum were on our itinerary. So much to see and only a day to take in all the sights and sounds of the city! We also rode the subway from Times Square to the Bowery, and I don't recall being afraid to go where we went.

Then it was on to Annapolis, Maryland, where we toured the U.S. Naval Academy, founded in 1845 by Secretary of the Navy George Bancroft in President James Polk's administration. The purpose was, and is, to train future officers for the U.S. Navy and Marine Corps. The campus covers 232 acres, the site of all the classrooms, administration buildings, dormitories, athletic facilities and drill fields. Most impressive is the academy chapel, dominated by three gigantic, artful stained-glass windows dedicated to the memory of Admirals Farragut, Porter and Sampson. Admiral John Paul Jones, father of the U.S. Navy, is entombed in the chapel at the academy, after having rested in an unmarked grave in Paris, France, for one hundred years. His two famous quotes are: "I have not yet begun to fight" and "In time of peace, prepare for war."

Visiting Washington, D.C., we viewed all the landmarks of our nation's capital that we had learned about in high school civics class, which taught how governments function. We saw all the traditional tourist attractions: the Lincoln Memorial, the Jefferson Memorial, the White House and the Washington Monument. Three or four of us who were on the school's cross-country team ran up the Washington Monument nonstop. After that feat, our 2.5-mile cross-country course was, in comparison, a stroll in the park.

Our visit to the J. Edgar Hoover Building, which houses the FBI, was very impressive, and our guide there was obviously a recent graduate of the FBI Academy. He showed us the forensic lab and how agents collect and analyze crime scene evidence and data. Row upon row of fingerprint records were on file. Keep in mind that in 1950, this data wasn't on computers.

Our young guide was quite authoritative, explaining how the information on criminals was catalogued on three-by-five filing cards. Approaching a filing cabinet, he announced with pride that these cards represented notorious and desperate criminals who had been apprehended and were doing prison time. "For example," he declared and, with a flourish, whipped out a file card, "Kate Ma Barker!"

With that, forty-two of us let out a howl of laughter. That wasn't a polite thing to do, but we couldn't help ourselves! We plead guilty on the basis of incongruity—the FBI, Ma Barker and our motherly chaperone? No way! (By coincidence, our chaperone's first name was Kay.) The hapless lad got all flustered and embarrassed. What in the world could be so humorous about a hardened criminal like Ma Barker and her gang of boys?

After we had bridled our boundless mirth and explained that our chaperone was referred to as "Ma Barker," he appreciated what the laughter was all about. With all the cards, it was just his luck to pick that particular one!

The tragic irony of the Ma Barker case is that she was not a criminal; she never participated in or organized a bank robbery, kidnapping or extortion. It was her four sons and members of the Karpis Gang who were the criminals. She did, however, aid and abet the Barker-Karpis Gang. Alvin Karpis, in his book *The Alvin Karpis Story*, stated, "Ma Barker was never a criminal and when we traveled together as a mother and her sons, what could look more innocent?" Harvey Bailey, a bank robber who occasionally pulled off jobs with the Barker-Karpis Gang, gave further evidence of Ma's innocence: "The old woman couldn't organize breakfast!" On January 16, 1935, FBI agents were attempting to arrest Ma Barker's son Fred at a Lake Weir cabin near Ocala, Florida. Both were killed in the shootout—Ma Barker by accident.

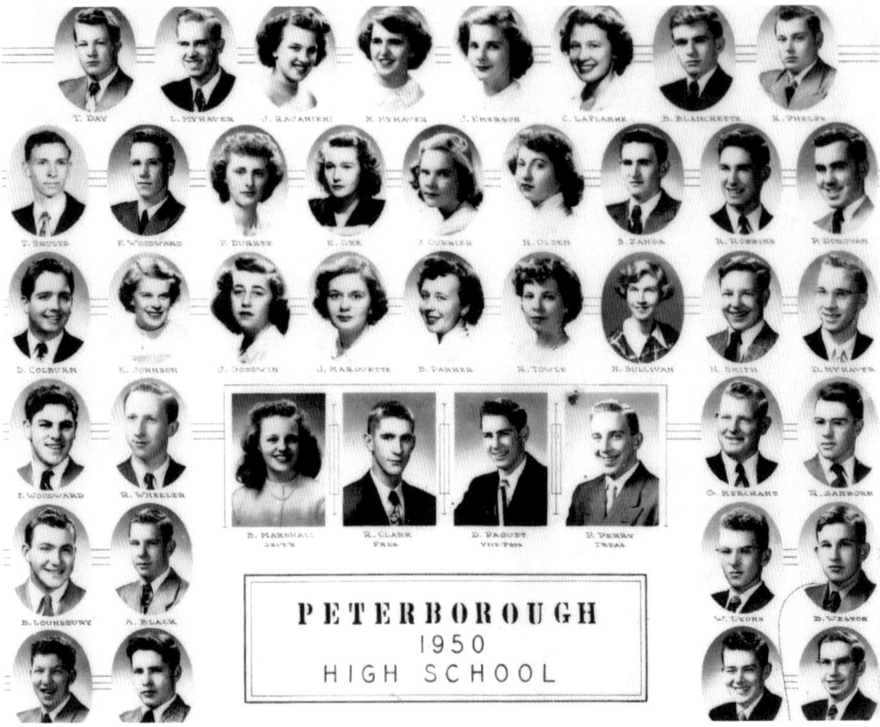

Here's to the class of 1950, Peterborough High School. You could not ask for better classmates. Our years together were enjoyable, memorable and educational. As we go our separate ways, may peace, happiness and good health follow us.

By all accords, the senior class trip of 1950 was an outstanding, enjoyable and educational event. We returned home with a better appreciation of our nation's capital. The only shenanigans we did was drop some water balloons out our New York City hotel room on hapless victims walking along the sidewalk five stories below.

Our Senior Prom and graduation in June would be the last two occasions when we would be together as the class of 1950, Peterborough High School. We would never see many of our forty-two classmates again, as we went our separate ways.

IN MEMORIAM

Abner Black joined the class of PHS 1950 in fifth grade at the Central School, coming from Dublin when that school closed. Upon graduation, Abner joined the U.S. Marine Corps. He was promoted to the rank of corporal, shipping out to the Korean War with Fox Company, Second Battalion, Fifth Marines, First Division (FMF). Corporal Black was a fire team leader, killed in action on Pork Chop Hill on March 29, 1953. He was awarded the Purple Heart, the Korean Service Medal and the United Nations Service Medal. *Semper fi*, Abner.

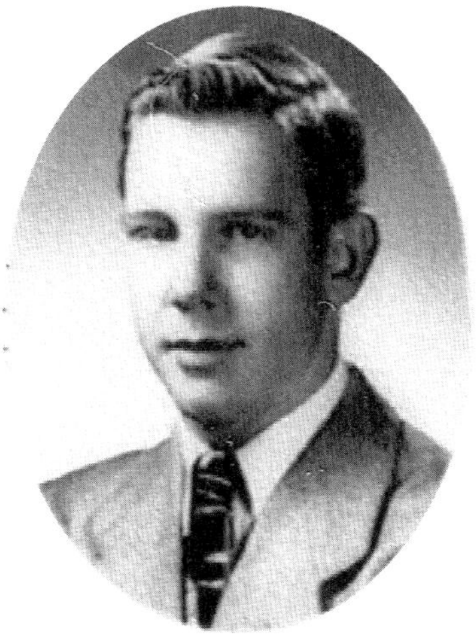

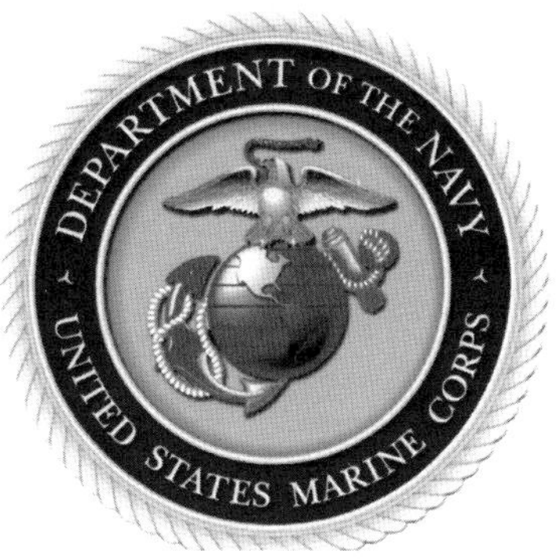

Above right: In memoriam: Corporal Abner Black, USMC.

Right: Marine Corps emblem.

Bibliography

Allen, Everett S. *A Wind to Shake the World Little*. Toronto, ON: Brown & Co. Boston, 1976.

Allen, Mel, ed. *Yankee Magazine*, September 2008.

Amidon, Cynthia. *Remembering Hancock*. Charleston, SC: The History Press, 2010.

Anderson, Peter. *Boston Globe*, June 21, 1978.

Boutwell, Iona. *Monadnock Ledger*, September 27, 1973.

Cohen, Stan. *The Tree Army: A Pictorial History of the CCC, 1933–42*. Missoula, MT: Pictorial History Pub. Co., 1980.

DeGregorio, William A. *The Complete Book of Presidents*. 5th ed. New York: Gramercy Books, 2002.

Encyclopedia Americana. Vols. 7–13, 15, 16, 18–23, 25–29. New York: American Corp, 1829–1956.

Fensterwald, John H., ed. Fletcher E. Dole obituary. *Monadnock Ledger*, May 21, 1980.

Historical Society of Cheshire County. Record Groups 3, 8, 9.

Josefsberg, Milt. *The Jack Benny Show*. New Rochelle, NY: Arlington House Publications, 1977.

Lehtinen, Alice E.E. *Peterborough Transcript*, March 29, 1973.

Morison, George Abbot. History of Peterborough, NH. Book I, *Narrative*. Book II, *Genealogies*. New York: Etta M. Smith and Richard R. Smith Pub., 1954.

Nash, J. Madeleine Smithsonian "Storm Warnings" September 2006

Nash, Jay Robert. *Look for the Woman*. New York: M. Evans & Co. Publisher, n.d.
Olson, T.M. *Elements of Dairying*. New York: Macmillan Co., 1950.
Page, Ralph E. *Night of Honor*. Historical Society of Cheshire County, n.d.
Pearson, Haydn S. *The New England Year*. New York: W.W. Norton & Co., 1966.
Peterborough Bicentennial Committee, 1976.
Peterborough Transcript. "Last Passenger Train." 1953.
Petersen W.E., Jr. *Dairy Science: It's Principles*. 2nd ed. Chicago: J.B. Lippincott Co., 1950.
Py-Lieberman, Beth. *Smithsonian* 32, no.11 (February 2002): 65.
Rumrill, Allan F. Historical Society of Cheshire County. Library Record Groups 3, 8, 9.
Shultz, Earl N. *The Centennial Year*. The American Guernsey Cattle Club, n.d.
Simmons, Edwin Howard, Robert Moskin, eds. *The Marines*. N.p.: Hugh Lautner Levin Assoc., 1998.
Van Der Vat, Dan. *Pearl Harbor: A Day of Infamy*. Paintings by Tom Freeman. Introduction by John McCain. Toronto: Madison Press Books, 2001.
Whittemore, Suzanne Bergeron. "In the Shadow of Monadnock." *Historic Towns Cheshire County*, n.d.
Wikipedia, s.v. "Dublin," "Francestown," "Greenfield," "Hancock," "Keene" and "Jaffrey." www.wikipedia.org.
Willits, C.O. *Agricultural Handbook No. 134, Maple Syrup Producers Hand Book*. Washington, D.C.: USDA, 1965.
The World Almanac and Book of Facts. New York: World Almanac Educational Group, Inc., 2004.

About the Author

Tom Shultz is a retired dairy farmer from Lowville, New York. He has written numerous short stories and magazine articles and enjoys reading and writing nonfiction. This is his first full-length book. Tom grew up in Peterborough, New Hampshire, and his time there set the direction for his life. After high school, he attended the University of New Hampshire, earning a bachelor's degree in dairy husbandry. After serving for three years in the United States Marine Corps, he received an honorable discharge with the rank of sergeant.

Tom graduated with a master's degree in dairy production from Kansas State University and was employed by the New York State Cooperative Extension Service. While on a farm visit to the owner of a Delaware County Jersey herd, he met his future wife, Peggy, one of the farmer's daughters.

After eleven years with Cooperative Extension, Tom fulfilled his dream of having his own dairy farm when he and Peggy bought a 120-acre farm in Lewis County, New York. With the able assistance of sons Mike, Joe, Jim and Tim, they operated a typical family dairy farm with thirty-six registered Holsteins. Upon retirement, he and Peggy sold the farm to their son Joe. Joe and his wife, Sue, now operate the farm with Tom and Peggy's grandson, Bronson.

Visit us at
www.historypress.net